When Swing Was King

Looking back at one of the most historical eras in America and American music.

ART KOCH

Published by Richter Publishing LLC www.richterpublishing.com

Editors: Monica San Nicolas

Formatted by: Diana Fisler

ISBN:0692581723
ISBN-13:9780692581728

DISCLAIMER

This book is designed to provide information on the history of swing bands only. This information is provided and sold with the knowledge that the publisher and author do not offer any legal or medical advice. In the case of a need for any such expertise, consult with the appropriate professional. This book does not contain all information available on the subject. This book has not been created to be specific to any individual's or organization's situation or needs. Every effort has been made to make this book as accurate as possible. However, there may be typographical and/ or content errors. Therefore, this book should serve only as a general guide and not as the ultimate source of subject information. This book contains information that might be dated and is intended only to educate and entertain. The author and publisher shall have no liability or responsibility to any person or entity regarding any loss or damage incurred, or alleged to have incurred, directly or indirectly, by the information contained in this book. You hereby agree to be bound by this disclaimer or you may return this book within the guarantee time period for a full refund. All characters appearing in this work are historical figures and author has made best attempts to recall certain events and situations as best as possible. Author make no claims as to the authenticity of the stories within this book. Any resemblance to other persons, living or dead, is purely coincidental. All photos used in this work are for demonstration and research purposes only and used with the fair use copyright act.

DEDICATION

I would like to dedicate this book to those who lived and served during this period in our history. I would also like to dedicate this book to those who came after this time period but were told about, and learned about what a historic time it was. I would also like to dedicate this book to the younger generation of today who, I hope, will learn something of what their grandparents and great grandparents went through both good and bad during those years. May you all take away some great memories from this book.

CONTENTS

INTRODUCTION

Throughout the history of the United States, music has always been a big part of the fabric that was woven to create the canvas that shaped this new country. There were the pristine moves of the minuet during the early days of our country's birth, and then the soulful and spiritual sounds of the black slaves. At the turn of century, there was the elegance and precision of the waltz. Again, the black people had their ragtime and blues music in the early 1900's. Then along came writers like Cohan, Berlin, and others with show tunes as the bright lights of Broadway glistened nightly with exciting musicals. Then it was time for the wild and crazy roaring '20's and the Charleston craze that was going on everywhere. Radio came into being and all kinds of music could be heard on this new medium. There was the popularity of country music in its early stages through the Grand Ole Opry. Along came a music explosion in the 1950's with the birth of "rock-and-roll", creating a sensation with teenagers against many odds. However, this music would be the sounding board for not only the '50's, but the '60's and beyond.

Yet with all that, there was one period of music that literally changed the entire musical direction of this country for a couple of reasons. First, it was something completely new sound wise, and second, because of the time period in which it took place, it would act as a bellwether for the entire country, what it had been through and what was ahead in the next decade. I am talking about the period of 1935 through 1947, known as the Big Band/Swing Era. This was a period in history and a style of music that, while not

aware of it then, came along at just the right time. With all the various forms of music society had been enjoying over the many decades as part of our American culture, none ever had the impact on people of all ages like that of the big band/swing era. The music these bands would play was a veritable smorgasbord of styles, tempos, rhythms, showmanship, and sheer enjoyment. It was music that people could really dance to, feel romantic, and hold each other close. They could also allow themselves to cut loose, letting their inhibitions go in the newest dance craze, the jitterbug. It was music that was serious but fun, and many of the bands would become a show in themselves the way they presented their music from the bandstand. The music was such that dance palaces, clubs, restaurants and ballrooms soon would be packed on any given night with people of all ages enjoying themselves. It came at a time when the country was trying its best to climb out of one of the worst depressions in history. In *1935*, as the country continued its struggle to get back on its collective feet, no one had any idea what would lie ahead in the coming year, let alone the coming decade. They say timing is everything, and this new style of music could not have come along at a better time.

The country had gone through Prohibition in the '20's and a time when the gangsters ran roughshod over the country with bloody battles taking place everywhere. Bonnie and Clyde, Luciano, Capone and others were constantly causing mayhem. The 1920's was also a period of great wealth and great excess leading to that fateful day, October 29, 1929, "Black Tuesday", when Wall Street crashed and everything came tumbling down like a house of cards. With literally the snap of a finger, millions upon millions were out of work, lost their homes, lost every dime they had, and were made stand in soup lines just to get something to eat. It was a devastating time in U.S. history. Because of the crash, over $25 billion (today that would be $369 billion) was lost and there was very little hope that things would change. It was a devastating time.

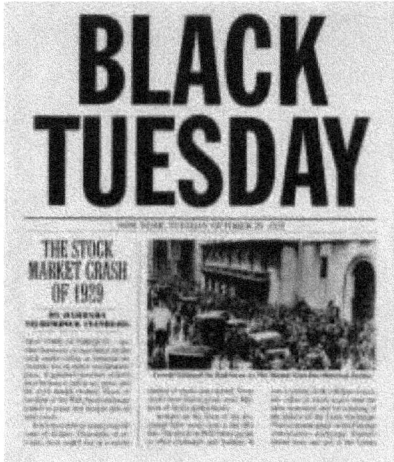

BLACK TUESDAY

THE STOCK MARKET CRASH OF 1929

Through all of the country's growing pains since the very beginning, Americans never lost their resolve. With the election of Franklin Delano Roosevelt as 32nd President, a state of normalcy would slowly begin to take place and the nation would see change for the better under his administration. Many of his new policies would have a lasting effect on the U.S. then and in the future. As they had in the past, America would stand tall, rebound, and rebuild itself better and stronger. By 1935, things began to look more promising. Roosevelt's programs like the New Deal and WPA put people back to work with a sense of security. Again the American people persevered, looking ahead to a brighter future and came together as one. The hope was that what happened on that fateful day of October 29, 1929 would be a great lesson and sounding board to never have something of that scope take place ever again.

The first four years of FDR's presidency saw things moving slowly but definitely on an upward and positive path. People believed in FDR and what he was doing to bring the country back stronger than before. The song *"Happy Days are Here Again"* became a very prominent tune and somewhat of an anthem of better times coming. At the same time, the U.S. was also aware of what was beginning to take place across the

Atlantic in Europe, but there was no reason for us to worry...or was there? No one at the time had any idea what we would be faced with when the decade of the 1940's came along. FDR, in one of his many famous "fireside chats", reassured the nation that there was nothing to worry or be concerned about. He said we would be just fine and our number one priority was the rebuilding of both the country and people's lives from the pitfalls of the depression. If the American people thought going through prohibition, the crash, and the devastating depression that followed was a tough road, what the 1940's had in store would really test our mettle and resolve as a country.

Enter the beginning of what was to become the big band/swing era.

CHAPTER 1
SWING BEGINS ITS FLIGHT
1935 – 1937

In *1935*, more and more people were getting back to work, lives and futures were being rebuilt, and the overall confidence level was very high. People were enjoying going to ballgames, movies, plays, and restaurants. They enjoyed evenings out dancing to the popular bands of the time that included the orchestras such as *Gus Arnheim* (future movie star *Fred MacMurray* was a sax player in the Arnheim band), *Ben Pollack*, *Paul Whiteman*, *Blue Barron*, *Guy Lombardo*, *Anson Weeks* (future Queen of the West, *Dale Evans* was the singer with the Weeks band) were some of the big favorites. These bands relied on mostly "sweet" music. Anything up-tempo was always played in a very safe manner and had strict appeal to an older crowd. It would be a young, bespectacled clarinetist who had played as a sideman in several bands, *Benny*

Goodman, who'd had a vision of changing the sound and style of music. He felt the time was right for a change and having a big swing band. Goodman's idea was met with a lot of resistance by club owners, and record people who felt it would serve little purpose in society. They reasoned that it was too different, too loud, and too fast. They said it was not what dancers wanted or needed. Goodman refused to take no for an answer and forged ahead, becoming the man responsible for what would be the beginnings of the big band/swing era. In reality and looking back, the timing for this change, regardless of the closed minds of restaurant and club owners as well as record labels, was perfect. The country was climbing out of a terrible depression and needed something new, different, exciting, and entertaining. Could this young, relatively unknown clarinet player actually open that door and have other bands follow his lead? Most everyone said no, it would never work, and many were very skeptical about this new music that **Benny Goodman** was about to unleash. After several years as a sideman in several bands, he was convinced it was time to take music in a whole new direction and was willing to stake his reputation on it. So, just how did this free-spirited, talented clarinet player bring this change about?

Goodman knew he had to have an exceptional group of musicians to get this off the ground, so he sought out a solid unit of musicians he'd worked with in other bands and studios. With no agent at the time, he booked his own engagements, and somehow was able to convince NBC

to give him a radio shot. They gave him a 30 minute slot at midnight one night a week, figuring it would have no audience and that they could go cancel him any time. When Goodman and his band began playing some dates, most didn't go that well at various clubs on the East Coast, so he made the decision that a trip out to the

West Coast was in order. When the band finally got to Los Angeles, they had a few hours to get ready for an engagement at the **Palomar Ballroom** in Los Angeles. What took place after the Goodman band began to play was quite a story. Because his radio broadcast went on the air at midnight in the east, it was only 9 o'clock in the west. Because of the time difference, Goodman's band had already created a big West Coast audience. The stint at the Palomar was jam-packed every night with folks—mostly younger—ready to dance to Goodman's new style of music in person, and they loved it. From the success of that engagement, and even more successful stops on the trip back to New York, Goodman's popularity quickly began to grow and would eventually create a momentous event that would give the Swing Era its place in American musical history. With all this new success coming Goodman's way, many of his critics were beginning to change their tune (pun intended). Even the very popular orchestra leader, **Paul Whiteman**, the potentate of jazz, took notice. A few years later, he would be very much involved.

As for the event that would take place shortly after Benny's success, it did not involve Goodman, at least not in the beginning. Against strong advice from music insiders, **Robert Weitman**, the manager of the famed **Paramount Theater** in New York City, booked **Glen Gray and his Casa Loma Orchestra** as an on-stage feature attraction between

the movies for two weeks. The Gray band wasn't really a sweet band, and it wasn't a swing band either, but more a solid combination of the two with very slick, polished, danceable arrangements. The band dressed in tuxedos and had a very elegant look. Everyone thought that

Weitman was out of his mind and the Paramount would be an empty theater. The New York newspapers, in particular the snobby *New York Times*, called the idea "a boorish, preposterous, nonsensical idea." Predictions ran rampant that this wondrous 3,500 seat theater would be lucky to have 100 people inside. What was the reasoning for the negativity by the newspapers? The main one was, why would people want to come to a theater see a movie, then sit and watch a band play on stage? Despite all this being written, Weitman was undaunted and positive it would work. He had checked out different clubs around New York and was well aware how people were catching onto this new swing music and enjoying it. Music insiders said it would be financial suicide for the famed theater. A club with a dance floor might be able to make it work, but not on the stage of a movie theater. However, like Goodman proved the critics wrong about swing music, Weitman was about to do the same with this bold, unprecedented move.

In their first week at the Paramount, the **Glen Gray Orchestra** set a house box office record and a 2-week engagement became 4 weeks! The concession stands were continually running out everything on a daily basis and box office receipts were the best they had ever been. Wagging their tails, most all the critics admitted they were wrong about Weitman's idea. The one critic who still felt it was a waste was the *New York Times*, but as the era would continue to grow, the *Times* would never give the big band/swing era and its players their due. Buoyed by this success with the Gray band, Weitman booked other bands to play at the Paramount on a regular basis. Seeing the success in New York, a few other theaters around the country jumped on the bandwagon, signing different bands to play at their theaters while on

tour. Many of the theaters enjoyed success with the bands' appearances. Among the new bands that began breaking in at the time was the *Dorsey Brothers Orchestra*, which Tommy and Jimmy had formed a year earlier after playing for various other bands. It was a solid unit with a subdued sound featuring Jimmy's fluid sax and Tommy's melodic trombone. The problem was the brothers never got along and engaged in verbal fights both on and off stage. One night it got so bad during an engagement that Tommy picked up his trombone walked off the bandstand, never to return. That brought an end to the two brothers leading what was a very good band with promise. Within days, Tommy would take over the remains of the *Joe Haymes Orchestra*, hire some top-tier musicians he was familiar with, as well as a young, extremely talented arranger named *Sy Oliver*. By mid-1935, the *Tommy Dorsey Orchestra* was born and gave dancers their brand of unique, very danceable swing music.

By this time, music critics for the most part, were convinced this new style of music was here to stay and would get bigger as more bands began to form and make their debuts at various clubs and dance

palaces, as well as radio. The two big music magazines, bibles of the industry, *Down Beat* and *Metronome*, began to follow the bands more closely. They reported on record sales, appearances, did reviews, interviews and even created a Top 10 chart.

Because of the change taking place, some of the sweet bands did their best to implement their versions of swing into their music libraries, but often with less-than-favorable results. One of the bands that did have some success by adding swing numbers was **The Kay Kyser Orchestra**. They not only played good dance music and had a popular radio show,

but also got their audience involved as well with their humorous *"Kollege of Musical Knowledge"* routine that was a part of every show they did both on radio and in person. Kyser made no bones about the fact that he wasn't crazy about the new swing sound, but he was also a smart enough businessman to know what would sell and made sure his arrangers added several good, danceable swing numbers to his catalog.

While swing was beginning to catch on from coast to coast, there were many other newsworthy events that took place in 1935 in the name of progress. The polygraph was invented, the first transatlantic postal service began, the DC-3 commercial airliner made its debut, and baseball great Babe Ruth retired from baseball. Nylon was created, the Boulder Dam was completed, and the U.S. Social Security was is signed into law by FDR. Ritz Crackers were in the stores, as well as Kit Kat candy bars. A new baking company called Pepperidge Farms came on the scene. As for radio entertainment, families gathered

around their radios to listen to **Fibber McGee and Molly**, **Flash Gordon**, **Fred Allen**, **Lux Radio Theater**, and others. When it came to movies, people found time to enjoy **Mutiny on the Bounty**, **Marx Brothers Night at the Opera**, **Bride of Frankenstein**, and **Captain Blood** to name a few. With many new inventions, new products, good entertainment of different kinds, and life slowly getting back to a more normal state, the people were beginning to have a very good feeling about the future. While there was still much to be done, Americans and government were committed to putting the Great Depression behind them and ready to move on to bigger, better years and decades ahead.

1936 would be the year when some top hotels around the country began switching music policies adding swing bands to their roster. One of them, the previously very staid and pompous **Madhattan Room** in the posh **Hotel Pennsylvania** in New York City previously only allowed for very monotone, tired society music. Now it became the new home for the **Benny Goodman Orchestra**, who played to a packed room every night. Forming their first swing bands in 1936 were **Artie Shaw** and **Charlie Barnet**, who quickly found audiences that liked their style of swing music at places like the **Rainbow Room**, **Roseland**, **Meadowbrook**, **Paradise Restaurant**, and other venues where people came to dine and dance. While radio had been broadcasting bands for a couple of years, with the exception of Goodman, it had been all sweet bands and local shows. Now networks saw the growing popularity of swing and the great commercial potential and money to be made. Bands began to get more airtime and their own shows. NBC began a 3-hour program called "Saturday Night Swing Session" that went on the air at 9 p.m. EST and went coast to coast. The show featured a mix of sweet and swing bands and quickly developed a huge following across the country. The show quickly increased the various bands visibility, record sales and personal appearances dramatically, making advertisers happy as well. It was just one more step in the right direction as far as the music. While swing was still in its infancy, there was no question now that Goodman had the right idea from the very beginning about this change.

Because the demand for records and sheet music was beginning to soar to new heights, bands were in the recording studios much more than previously. The early beginnings of the big band/ swing era was not only becoming a big boon to clubs, restaurants and ballrooms, but also the record labels, sheet music publishers and commercial sponsors of the radio shows. It also brought about new management and booking firms that would increase the number of bookings bands were getting and increase the band's pay as well. This new found popularity for big band swing music would also create one more opening for this music's popularity. It would be an opening that would have a very big effect on its continued growing fan base.

We are referring to a number of other bands who, because of discrimination, could now finally play for white audiences instead of just black audiences. It now meant everyone, black or white, could hear any number of the stylish black dance bands like *Chick Webb* (with very

young *Ella Fitzgerald* as his female vocalist), *Jimmy Lunceford, Count Basie, Benny Moten, Duke, Ellington, Erskine Hawkins, Don Redman, Isham Jones* and the very impressive showman/singer/orchestra leader *Cab Calloway*, who all found new audiences to play for. These bands were now able to play at the better clubs and ballrooms, as well as doing radio and getting bigger record sales. It was a huge step forward, but because of discrimination there were still some roadblocks. On the road, they could only stay at all black hotels, eat at black only restaurants and worst of all, the lack bands got paid less than the white bands even though they packed the venues, but that was how it was done back then. Discrimination aside, with the black bands now part of swing's growth, the cross section of music became even broader with so many different danceable styles to choose from and enjoy. While big band/swing music was putting the country in a great frame of mind and its popularity continued to grow, a few critics wondered if it would last beyond a couple years then die out. What they, as well as the fans, didn't know was the best of this new style of music was yet to come.

There were a lot of other happenings taking place in 1936. People began to hear more rumblings across the Atlantic and the new leader in Germany, Adolf Hitler, who was totally obsessed with maniacal power. In addition, Ethiopia was invaded by the Italian dictator Mussolini. There was a civil war going on in Spain and the Germans and Japanese would sign an anti-Communist agreement forming the Axis which would create big problems worldwide. While the American public was aware of this from radio news reports, newspapers and newsreels, FDR would continue to assure everyone during his fireside chats the country had nothing to worry about. The U.S. would remain neutral as it was not our war to fight. Good times were on the way back and a feel of prosperity began to become more evident. The outlook of an exciting future lay ahead and FDR wanted the country to concentrate in the positives of what the future held for the country.

Theaters, ballrooms, clubs and restaurants saw big financial returns with the growing interest in swing bands. Radio networks added more band shows and even had announcers playing records a couple of hours during the day. That was another offshoot of the big band/swing movement we will touch on later. Record labels signed new bands who were in the studio more than before. When it came to movie theaters, the Paramount was now considered the number one theater for a band to appear in. Quite a change from 2 years earlier when everyone thought Robert Weitman's idea was crazy. However, what took place at the Paramount when the **Benny Goodman Orchestra** opened there cemented the popularity not only of Goodman, but bands playing on a theater stage as well. On March 3, 1937, a light snow fell and temperatures were below freezing in New York City. Yet at 7 a.m. people—mostly teens—were lined up four and five deep around the block waiting to get into the Paramount when it opened at 9 a.m.! The theater would remain packed all day and night. The fans were happy, they danced in the aisles, concession stands going full blast, and the Paramount was setting box office records day after day. It would be just one of many events to come that would prove just how far reaching this new music style was.

Ozzie Nelson   *Charlie Barnet*   *Artie Shaw*

By now, other bands were getting noticed and becoming part of the scene. **Charlie Barnet**, **Artie Shaw**, **Bunny Berigan**, **Ted Weems** (with a young singer by the name of **Perry Como**) and Ozzie Nelson (yep, future rock idol **Rick Nelson's** dad) among the newer bands. All of them, besides solid club dates, were eager to take to the Paramount stage as Gray, Goodman, Dorsey and others had done successfully. It was during

this time several future band leaders were either sidemen in other bands, arrangers for a band or a session musicians in the recording studios. One of them was a young trombonist who was both sideman and arranger. He was handpicked by British band leader **Ray Noble** to assemble an American band for him. The trombonist/arranger's name was **Glenn Miller**. The Noble band assembled by Miller would have great success for a number of years. Putting that band together gave Miller the idea he could put his own group together. In 1937, Miller's first band took to the road and it was a total disaster. So much so, that Miller was convinced that leading a band was not for him and decided that he'd stick to arranging and being a sideman. However, thanks to his bride Helen, best friend and piano player Chummy McGregor and a Boston ballroom operator by the name

of **Sy Schribman** convinced him to not give it up. They all felt he could make it work and that the time was right. So, Miller gave in, reforming the band to give it one more shot. It would take a little time but once the name

Ray Noble's Rainbow Room Orchestra 1935
Glenn Miller and Charlie Spivak standing in rear

11

Nation's
Loneliest Man

became known the overall impact the ***Glenn Miller Orchestra*** would have on the big band/swing era would escalate into big historical proportions no one could have ever imagined or expected to see take place. We get into the emergence of Glenn Miller and the impact he and his band would have on the big band/swing era in our next segment.

Just like today, and any other period of music, not everyone was thrilled with this movement toward swing. Lovers of the sweet, society music sound, classical, opera and Broadway felt the music was "savage", "immoral", and would lead to a moral downfall of the young people. They wanted it stopped before it ruined the youth. How ironic that just 20 years later, the same things would be said about a new form of music called rock-and-roll. Yet, here we are today in 2015, some 70 plus years later, still functioning, still growing, still listening to all kinds of musical styles and our lives continue to go on. Back then in answer to the criticism, one bandleader took on the "music snobs" and said, "One day the big bands and swing are going to be playing on classical music's turf." It was a very bold statement to make with swing still in its infancy. Of course this band leader was laughed at for making the comment, but his words would prove to be very prophetic.

The country was continuing to move away from the depression and paid little attention to what was taking place in Europe. FDR had instilled a new faith in the American people regarding progress and a bright future. His New Deal

was in place, he had signed on the Social Security act, people were back at work on a steady basis, and the economy was showing signs of recovery. Between 1935-1937, many new additions came along. The public got their first glance at *Look Magazine*, comic book followers had a new hero called Batman, and homemakers loved the new Betty Crocker products. The Mars Bar and Kraft Mac and Cheese made their debuts in 1937 and there were the first sales of Girl Scout cookies. Bandleader **Fred Waring's** new invention for the kitchen, the Waring Blender, also went on the market. Two huge building projects were also completed in 1937, the Golden Gate Bridge in San Francisco and the Lincoln Tunnel that linked New York and New Jersey both opened to traffic. There was major tragedy when the German airship, Hindenburg, crashed and burned at Lakehurst, N.J. The country also mourned the loss of the celebrated female pilot Amelia Earhart and actress Jean Harlow.

In addition to the big bands and music shows on radio, listeners had

plenty of other entertainment with **Fred Allen**, **Amos n' Andy**, **Jack Benny**, **Fibber McGee and Molly**, **The Shadow**, **Edgar Bergen & Charlie McCarthy**, **The Chase and Sanborn Hour** and something new for the ladies, daytime serials, which became better known as **soap operas** because the first sponsors of these new shows were the big soap companies. Who knew then seventy five years later they would be a staple of daytime TV? When it came to going to the movies in 1937 folks enjoyed great films like **Topper**, **The Good Earth**, **Captains Courageous**, **Lost Horizon**, and Disney's **Snow White and the Seven Dwarves**. It was quite a year for Hollywood not only because of some hit films, but three newcomers who made their film debuts in 1937. These men would go on to become three of the biggest legends of all time in films, **Cary Grant**, **Clark Gable**,

13

and *John Wayne*.

In the first two years of the swing/big band era, everything looked as if it was all headed on the right path to prosperity, with the bad times behind and only an exciting future ahead. By 1937, there was no doubting this "new" music had a lot to do with how people were feeling and reacting to life in general. It was also a good sign to see that most critics coast to coast from two years earlier had changed their minds and now staunch supporters of these talented musicians, bands and singers. It was also a good sign that in this short time that radio saw the potential of all of the different bands, not just the regional or sweet bands. The music landscape was bringing a different tune to the party. Just about everywhere you went, there was nothing but a positive aura as the hopes, dreams, and plans for the country's future now seemed untouchable.

CHAPTER 2
1938 – 1940
BIG BAND/SWING GROWS UP!

By *1938*, the big band/swing movement was moving into high gear. While the music's followers were mostly the teens and early twenties crowd, some older folks were beginning to really enjoy it as well. No longer were the sweet bands the only thing older people wanted to dance and listen to, there was room for both. Coast to coast, whenever a band appeared at a venue, it was always packed with a good cross-section of patrons. Radio expanded shows with a few bands even doing live remotes from the clubs, restaurants, and ballrooms where they were appearing. The majority of the big band radio shows began between 10 o' clock and midnight on the East Coast. People tuned in on Friday and Saturday nights in record numbers to listen and dance to their favorite bands. This also

brought another big plus, with the sales of records and sheet music hitting an all-time high. Several ballrooms like the **Aragon Ballroom** in Chicago got the brilliant idea to make even more money on a bands appearance. They would sell the bands records, sheet music and photos and offer a 50/50 split with the band. This would be the first time venues began selling an artist's product, long before it became a big business in the 1970's and 80's with rock concerts. Other places like restaurants, clubs and theaters were also feeling the windfall in big numbers that often doubled or tripled from the year before.

Yet with all positives, people's lives getting back on track and what the future held, across the Atlantic it was totally different. The top newscasters such as H. V. Kaltenborn, Edward R. Murrow, Lowell Thomas, and others kept people informed about Hitler and his running roughshod over Europe. FDR, now in his second term, always kept the outlook positive, telling America they were fine and would not get involved. The people had an unwavering faith in the president and went about their daily lives not concerned about what was taking place 6,000 miles away. That would dramatically change when, on October 30, 1938, America, coast to coast, got a very big

scare—not from Hitler—but from...men from Mars? On this Sunday night, a very talented 24-year old writer/director/actor by the name of **Orson Welles** presented his weekly dramatic show the **Mercury Theater on the Air**. On this night's program because it was the day before

Halloween, Welles presented his version of the H. G. Wells classic *"War of the Worlds"*. There was the disclaimer before the show to let the listeners know it was a fiction story. But Welles and his group of four actors, as well as a few people handling sound effects and music, made this program so realistic in every way that millions of people all over the country really did think we were being invaded by Martians. People fled in their cars, packed up belongings, left their homes to head for places where they would be safe. This created massive traffic jams everywhere, extra police were called out to handle panicking crowds and traffic. People were beside themselves not sure what the "Martians" were up to and why they were "invading" us. I was 3 years old at the time, but remember that night as if it happened yesterday and how my family reacted. Like most, they were packing things, getting me out of bed, getting in the car and heading up to the Catskill Mountains to escape this coming terror from outer space and seek safe refuge in the country. Of course, later it was all found to be Welles fictional radio show, but the panic and problems it caused everywhere even led to some lawsuits that were either settled or tossed out of

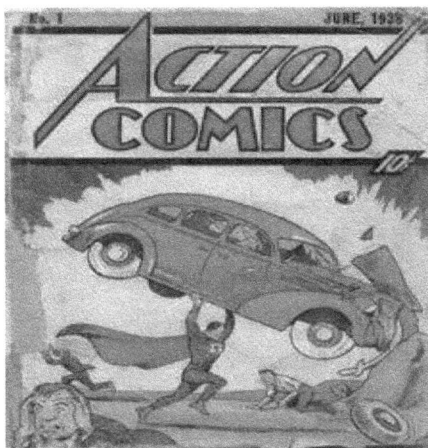

court. As for the show itself, many experts have said, and I totally agree, that Welles presentation was, and is, the greatest radio program of all time.

Before we get into more of the growth of the bands during this year, there were other great happenings taking place in 1938. The luxury liner *Queen Elizabeth* was launched, Howard Hughes set a new round-the-world flight record and a new comic book hero called *"Superman"* makes its debut. It was also the year the ball point pen was first marketed, Bumble Bee Tuna came on the market and instant coffee is introduced by Nescafe. FDR signs a new law raising the minimum wage from 25 cents to 40 cents an hour. Moviegoers were treated to great films like *Angels with*

Dirty Faces, *Boys Town*, *Jezebel*, *You Can't Take it With You* and it was the first year of a new movie cartoon character, *Bugs Bunny*.

On radio, there were plenty of choices between music, drama, comedy, serials and also the debut of *Kate Smith's* stirring version of *"God Bless America"* on her weekly show. The song would quickly become the country's second unofficial anthem, and is considered such to this day.

When it came to the big bands, one of the more successful new ones was *Artie Shaw's*, but one day he just up and quit and went to Mexico. A few months later he would return, completely revamp his band and became an even bigger hit. There was also a young musician from Duke University who burst on the scene with a new,

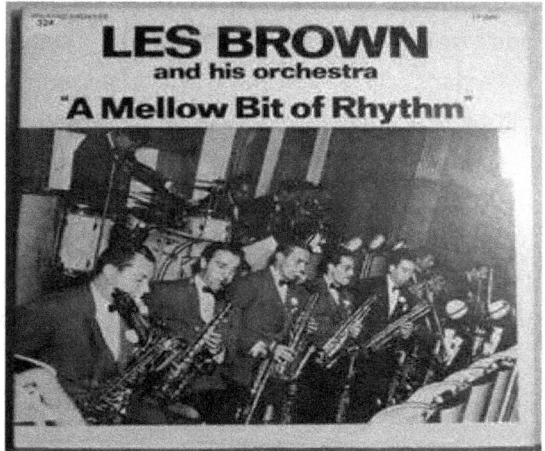

young band. They were playing a summer engagement at the *Pavilion at Budd Lake*, New Jersey drawing great crowds every weekend and most nights. When the summer was over, most of the musicians headed back to Duke to finish their education. However, the leader and a couple of his sidemen decided to stay. He put a whole new band together and from that point on, the *Les Brown Orchestra* would become a major part of the big band era and well beyond. In Brown's case his hookup with *Bob Hope* on radio and USO tours during WW II, then television later made the Brown band one of the best-known and popular for many years. Even after the big band scene had faded away, Brown's band not only was a staple with Hope, but also playing as many as 150 concert dates a year until Brown retired in the '70's.

Charlie Barnet and his band was also getting more and more popular with several hit records and packed dance clubs. Not only did he have a great swing band, but also some great vocalists. At one point Barnet was the first white band to use a black female singer when the exquisite and elegant *Lena Horne* was the vocalist for a time. It was also the year where the very popular *Benny Goodman* would be the first band to integrate when both pianist *Jess Stacey* and vibraharpist *Lionel Hampton* signed on with Benny. A few more of the sweet bands tried to implement swing into their music libraries but with mixed results. One "sweet" band that did quite well when it came to adding some swing numbers was the *Hal Kemp Orchestra* (future movie star *Janet Blair* sang with the Kemp band). As we mentioned earlier, *Kay Kyser* also did well adding some swing numbers that went over well. It is also interesting to note that the Kyser band also had two future stars as the vocalists. One was a future movie star *Jane Russell*, and the other a future TV talk show host, *Mike Douglas*.

The biggest addition to the list of new bands to come along in 1938 was *Glenn Miller*. After his disastrous 1937 attempt, Miller gave it one more shot. With radio at its peak, record and sheet music sales were at their highest. The dance clubs and ballroom were full. Miller was determined to make it work this time. He was a perfectionist, and a tough, but fair task master. He knew that in order to be successful and stand out, his new band needed something different from the others. It needed a "hook", but just what that was, Miller wasn't sure. He continued to try a variety of different

instrument combinations but none seemed to work and have a sound that would be different. It would take a freak accident at a band rehearsal that would, in turn, create what would soon become known as the "Miller sound". It came from having a clarinet lead over the sax section, something never done before and definitely a risk. Miller liked the combination and kept his fingers crossed that it would work. The band went through exhausting rehearsals to get this new sound right and then embarked on a cross country tour. Miller had gotten some airtime on the radio, even before he found "the sound" that resulted in a number of bookings. The band was still experimenting with the new sound on their tour and dancer reactions were good but nothing spectacular. Miller completely believed in this sound, continuing to tweak it here and there. As I mentioned, Miller was a perfectionist, but very fair and had the respect of all his musicians. He not only expected perfection in their playing, but in appearance, showmanship, and giving people more than just music. He wanted his band and singers to be a show within a show. With each live performance the entire Miller aggregation knew they were on to something good with this new sound. They knew the sound would pay off and set them apart from the pack and they gave Glenn nothing less than 100% every time out. Soon the big payoff on the "Miller sound" was about to take place.

On their opening night at the *Glen Island Casino* in New Rochelle, N.Y., the place was jam-packed. The band opened with what would become the most famous theme song of all time *"Moonlight Serenade"*, which Glenn had arranged himself. Halfway through the song, the dancers just stopped dancing and kept moving closer to the bandstand. Miller had a look of worry, when suddenly the Casino erupted in wild

The GLENN MILLER Orchestra

Live at the Glen Island Casino 1938

A COLLECTION OF COMPLETE UNEDITED AUDIO BROADCASTS

20

whistles and applause as the band continued to play the opening theme. The look on Miller's face, and those in the band, went from worry to smiles. The "Miller sound" was a huge hit. From that point on the **Glenn Miller Orchestra** would become the most recognized and most popular band of not only the big band/swing era, but of all time in the U.S. and around the world. In 1954, Hollywood paid homage to Miller by making the **"Glenn Miller Story"** *Jimmy Stewart* played Miller in a terrific role and **June Allyson** played his wife Helen. The film itself would nominated for an Oscar for the music and become a classic Hollywood film. It should be noted here that the role of Miller's boyhood best friend and piano player, Chummy McGregor, was played by **Harry Morgan**, who would become better known years later as Col. Potter on the hit TV series **"M*A*S*H"**. Hollywood did take a little liberty with the movie, but with Miller's widow, Helen, overseeing the script and also having final approval, plus the real Chummy McGregor as the film's technical advisor, 90% of what was in the film was factual. When it was released all the movie theaters were jam-packed to see this story about one of the greatest names in music history. To show the impact of Miller, the movie audience was made up of every age group from teens to senior citizens. It was also a smart move on the part of the film's producers to get as many of the original Miller band members and other name musicians possible to be in the band sequences. The film was nominated for three Oscars and won for best musical score, which was composed by a relative unknown back then, **Henry Mancini**.

It should be said here that back when all the bands were traveling the country on tour it was far from glamorous. My dad was part of that scene for a couple of years, but gave up being on the road, settling back down in New Jersey to put together his own band playing the tristate area.

In the '30's and '40's there were no super highways, 4- and 6-lane interstates, no Holiday Inns or Marriotts. The buses they traveled in were cramped, had little or no heat or air conditioning and usually had as many as two dozen or so people, plus all the instruments, bandstands, clothes, etc., traveling in every kind of weather. They battled snowstorms, rainstorms, heat, humidity, bitter cold and a lot more. In some case, bands traveled in a car caravan and had no bus. Many times they would pull into the town they were playing that night with just a couple of hours to spare, grab a quick bite to eat, set up, change clothes and be ready to play beginning at eight or nine o'clock. It was a tough life, but these men were dedicated to the music they loved, enjoyed what they did and in many cases got paid very well for their work. Miller and Dorsey were two of the best paying bands and why so many musicians stayed with them for years. Most bands liked staying together and being able to form a special chemistry, but illness, the military, getting married, or getting a better offer were about the only things that would create an opening for other musicians to hopefully fill.

There was also one other major event that would take place in early 1938 that would solidify the big band era with just about everyone. A few years earlier many of the music snobs had put down swing music as being savage and barbaric with no merit like opera or classical. It was **Benny Goodman** who had made the bold comment a couple years earlier that one day swing music would be played on their turf. In 1938, that is exactly what happened when Goodman put on his now famous Carnegie Hall Concert. Everyone told Benny it was a crazy idea, it would be committing musical suicide, he would be the butt of jokes and no one would bother to show up. His manager, **John Hammond**, was also a music critic and record producer who had a lot of "ins". He also believed this concert would work and prove swing music could be played

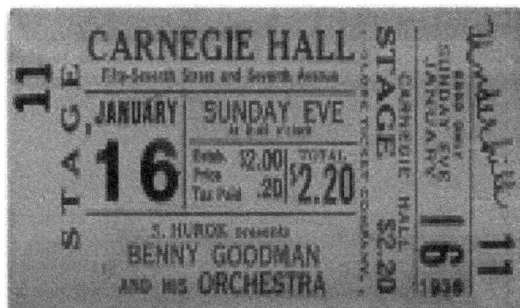

anywhere and even the most devoted fans of classical and opera could find enjoyment in this form of music. So with Hammond's backing, on January 16, 1938, Goodman took on Carnegie Hall and what took place on that night would become not only historic, but a game changer as well. The night of the concert it was very cold, temps were in the 20's with snow flurries, and this famed, historic hall was filled with a crowd aged over 50, composed of high-society men, all dressed in top hats and tails, and women in gowns and furs, who were dripping in diamonds, all sitting stiffly in their seats as the concert began. The first few songs drew only polite applause, but the band kept on going. Suddenly, things began to change and the audience began change their mood. Goodman quickly changed the order of songs

and moved up *"Sing, Sing, Sing"* in the order. Once this 7-minute long song got going, he had the entire audience clapping, stomping their feet, whistling and cutting loose. When the band

finished the song, the Carnegie Hall audience was on their feet, applauding Benny and his band. After that, the rest of the night went extremely well. When the band's final note of the evening played the applause lasted a good five minutes before Goodman and his band could get off the stage. It was a historic moment in this hallowed hall of classical and opera greats that changed the attitude of many more people, people of influence, people of means and gave the big band/swing era another big push.

The reviews in all the New York papers were extremely favorable and heaped high praise on the concert, with the exception of—who else— the *New York Times*. Their major review consisted of one line, "Goodman and his band a total bore." In spite of the *Times*, the recording of that concert by Columbia Records, first in 78 rpm form and then transferred to LP album form in the 1950's, would go on to become one of the best-selling albums of all time. Today, now in a 4-disc CD set, it still sells well. Try as they might the Times could never sway swing lovers to their way of thinking. The Times would never promote the big band/swing music as acceptable. The fact was after this very historic concert, several of these high society types were so impressed with the music and musicians that they used their own money to help a few new bands get started. When word of the Carnegie Hall concert spread around the country, other cities with big music halls wanted to do the same, but how do you top Carnegie Hall? Very simply, you don't. By now, the ballrooms and dance clubs roster was continuing to grow. In addition to places we have already mentioned, there was the **Aragon**, **Coconut Grove**, **Trianon**, **Palladium**, **Elitch Gardens**, **Walled Lake Casino**, **Seiler's Acres**, **The Coliseum**, **Rustic Cabins**, **Castle Farms**, **Savoy Ballroom**, **Starlite Room**, **Blackhawk Restaurant** and so many more throughout the entire country becoming the new havens for dancers and their unabashed love for the big bands and swing music.

The year *1939* would see many changes taking place here and abroad. The big bands were on the way to reaching their highest peak yet and

more new bands joined the parade. These included Will Bradley, *Jan Savitt*, *Larry Clinton*, *Claude Thornhill*, and the brother of crooner Bing Crosby, and *Bob Crosby* and his band. They all enjoyed success both in person and with record sales. The economy continued on a steady upswing as memories of the depression of ten years earlier were now seen as a bad memory. Detroit was kept busy producing sleek new automobiles and employment was at its highest peak in the decade.

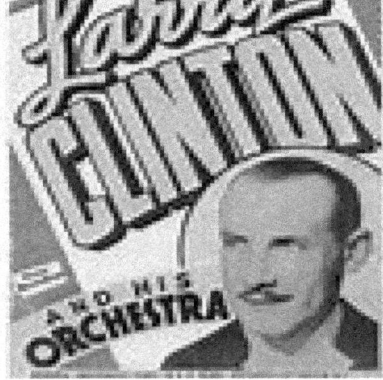

People were able to get a look at what the future would hold with the coming of the *1939-1940 New York World's Fair*. I was a wide-eyed child and marveled at everything I saw. I can still remember the huge exhibit they had called the *"World of Tomorrow"*, showing in detail what life in the U.S. would be like in the 1970's. Of everything that was shown, displayed and demonstrated, 90% of it had become reality by decade of the '70's. The pressure cooker was a new device for the kitchen and among new foods in 1939 were Lay's potato chips and Sara Lee cakes. Another construction marvel opened in 1939, the incredible Rockefeller Center Rink. Hollywood kept people entertained with great films that included *Goodbye Mr. Chips*, *Stagecoach*, *The Wizard of Oz*, and the sprawling Civil war drama, *Gone With the Wind*. In addition to big band radio shows there was a lot of variety with shows like Jack Benny, *Edgar Bergen*, *Bob Hope*, *The Lone Ranger*, *Grand Central Station*, *The Aldrich Family*, *Mr. District Attorney*. Daytime radio became even more popular with the ladies as a couple of new soap operas hit the airwaves. As for comic book lovers, *Dick Tracy* went from a newspaper comic strip to his own comic book and a new hero called the *Human Torch* also came on the scene. Sports fans filled the ballparks for baseball, enjoyed the cold weather of football, spent money at the race track and the boxing matches. Life, for the most part, seemed back on track with nothing but good times ahead.

As for the big bands and swing, 1939 would become its biggest year yet. Much of the success of '39 revolved around the music of the **Glenn Miller Orchestra**. As great as the established bands of **Dorsey**, **Shaw**, **Goodman** and others were doing, Glenn Miller and his new sound had literally taken the music world by storm.

The band dates at clubs, ballrooms and elsewhere were sellouts, his radio show had a huge audience, the recordings were selling faster than any other band and sheet music for Miller songs sold at an unprecedented rate. To further illustrate the band's overwhelming popularity, in the **Downbeat Magazine** poll, he was voted #1 by a unanimous margin and in the magazine **Metronome** he was voted the #1 swing band **AND** #1 sweet band. A new magazine called **Swing** also had the band listed as #1. By the end of 1939 the Miller band had netted 17 Top 10 songs, 6 number #1 hits, and another 5 songs in the Top 20. Miller's success also was a big help in elevating the overall popularity of the other bands in person and on recordings. Now, regardless of age, everyone was getting into the music in a very big way. Radio advertisers were thrilled with the audiences the networks were getting for the big band shows, and ballrooms coast to coast were packed every single weekend. It was not

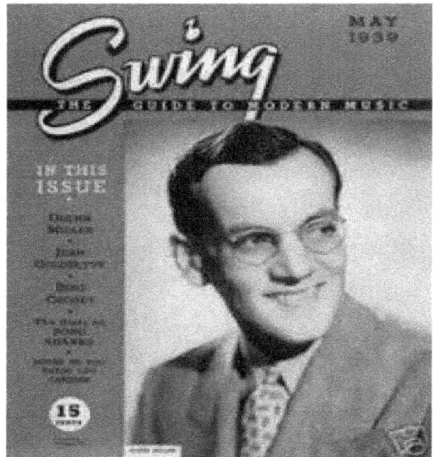

uncommon to see lines of people down the block waiting for the ballroom doors to open for a jam-packed evening of dancing and good times with a wide cross section of couples.

There was a very special event that would take place in 1939 that would further cement the big band era and encourage more new bands to get in on the music. The respected bandleader **Paul Whiteman** organized and presented another swing concert at Carnegie Hall. Unlike the Goodman concert in 1938, this crowd was made up of every age and they were ready right from the start to have a great time. Whiteman presented his own band, **Goodman**, **Fred Waring** and would end the concert with **Glenn Miller**. Whiteman acted as the emcee for the show as well. From the opening song from Whiteman's band, through their big set, Waring and Goodman's there was no question about the crowd reaction. The audience was continually very enthusiastic and responsive to the variety they witnessed. There was some dancing in the aisles that ushers didn't try to stop. After a short intermission, Mr. Whiteman took to the stage, smiled and simply said, "Ladies and gentlemen, our final band of the evening, Glenn Miller." Before he could get the name out, as the stage curtains parted, a jam-packed Carnegie Hall was on their feet applauding the band as they opened with a short version of their *"Moonlight Serenade"* theme, then went into *"A String of Pearls"* and took off from there. When the concert ended, the crowd applauded and milled around for a good 5 minutes before leaving the famed hall. The reviews in all of the New York papers were outstanding and praising everyone, except the *Times*, of course. They felt that respected men like Whiteman and Waring had lowered themselves to be associated with such barbaric noise. But music lovers, band leaders, singers, clubs,

theaters etc. got used to the Times and their disdain for the swing/big band era. It got to a point where the Times was not welcome at many big band appearances. The Times would only cater to the likes of Guy Lombardo, Carmen Cavallero, Sammy Kaye; bands with the sweet sound. Those feelings of the Times made little or no difference as the big band/swing era was forging ahead. The loss of one newspaper's backing meant little. Wherever the Miller band went, they were treated like the Beatles of the 1960's. In truth, Miller's band were the first pop superstars in music long before Elvis, the Beatles, Michael Jackson, etc.

As for radio, Miller was so popular on various shows that NBC gave the band their own show on Saturdays.

To top it all off, Hollywood was paying close attention to Miller. Hollywood had used some bands, but only in film shorts or for one musical number in a film and nothing more. They were never part of the story, no lines, no acting, just play one, maybe two numbers and nothing else. Now some Hollywood studio heads were seeing how much Miller could help a film, but he wasn't interested and turned down repeated offers. They continued to court him, but he continued to say no. The day would come when Miller and Hollywood would get together, but it would be on his terms only. In the meantime, they got other bands to continue to make their cameo appearances in films. Of course, being in a movie, even for just one or two songs, did help record and sheet music sales as well as personal appearances. For the most part the bands were happy with the arrangement because having to be on a set for only one day didn't cut into their appearance schedule. The other benefit was the bands were paid extremely well for their brief on camera appearances. Some questioned Miller and why he didn't give in to Hollywood, especially since the money was so good. He knew what it was that he wanted from Hollywood and what it would take, and he was more than willing to wait for it.

As the established swing and sweet bands continued to play on radio, appear in clubs, theaters and ballrooms with solid record sales there were a number of new bands who also began making their mark in 1939. They included **Alvino Rey and his Orchestra**, which featured Rey's "talking guitar", **Tony Pastor** featuring **The Clooney Sisters** (Rosemary would become a recording star in the 1950's), and through the backing of Miller the **Charlie Spivak Orchestra** made its debut with good success. There was also an excellent swing band led by trumpeter/singer **Vaughn Monroe** and two bands that came under the direction of two former Benny Goodman sidemen, drummer **Gene Krupa** and trumpeter **Harry James**. Krupa did well for a few years before returning to again being one of the era's best drummers. He did introduce the world to singer **Anita O' Day**. On the other hand, James was an instant hit with his great mix of hot swing numbers and very danceable romantic songs. He had assembled a very smooth aggregation of musicians, led by James sweet and swingy trumpet. But one of the main reasons for his instant success was his hiring of a young singing waiter he had taken notice of one night while having dinner at the **Rustic Cabins** in Fort Lee, New Jersey. He offered the waiter a job with the band as the vocalist and hired him on the spot. His name was **Frank Sinatra**.

As the country moved into the new decade in **1940**, the previous 10 years had seen many changes taking place, mostly good in many ways. People were working, the economy was getting better, families were closer, people, enjoyed going to

movies, restaurants, dances, sporting events. There were new modern products and inventions that had come along. FDR had been overwhelmingly elected to a third term as president and the outlook for the future was eagerly anticipated. The second year of the *1939-40 World's Fair* shattered attendance records as people flocked from all over the country to get a glimpse of what the future held. At the same time, big trouble escalated in Europe and in the Far East trouble was brewing there as well. While we were kept informed by news reports, newspapers, and newsreels of what was taking place, no one believed it was of any threat to us. FDR would continue to assure the American people we would remain neutral and not be involved in the battles taking place in Europe, but would supply our allies with whatever they were in need of. The country was relieved to know we were just helping our allies and our future was secure. In 1940 the entire U.S. military force totaled but 300, 000 and our Army Air Force was relatively nonexistent. Politicians felt having a heavily manned air force, and the expense to the American taxpayer, was not needed or even necessary. But that thought process would change. FDR signed into law the first peace time draft which was considered as nothing more than a way to bolster our own military not out of fear of what was happening in Europe. Young men wasted no time signing up for the draft doing their patriotic duty. In 1940, a new law was also passed making the 40-hour work week mandatory and anyone working more than 40 hours would be paid overtime wages. The majority of auto plants, mills, factories, etc. didn't mind this as long as it meant getting products out to the consumer as well as anything the military needed as

quickly as possible. With this new law, workers welcomed the chance to get some overtime, adding a few extra dollars to their paychecks.

For the most part, people were going about their everyday lives in a normal way enjoying the variety of entertainment that was popular at the time. In 1940 the big film hits included Disney's *Pinocchio* and *Fantasia*, dramas like *The Grapes of Wrath*, the big slap in the face to Hitler by Charlie Chaplin, *The Great Dictator*, and others. On radio, people listened to *Hope, Benny, Allen* and shows like *Abbott and Costello, Gene Autry's Melody Ranch, Dick Tracy, Jack Armstrong, Major Bowes Original Amateur Hour*, and of course, the ladies now had their soap operas, like *Our Gal Sunday* and *The Romance of Helen Trent*. 1940 was also the year in which a new vehicle called the Jeep made its debut, and how important that would become. The huge luxury liner *Queen Elizabeth* sailed into New York just for safekeeping while war escalated in Europe and Great Britain. A new sweet candy treat, M & M's was introduced and the very first *Dairy Queen* opened in Joliet, Illinois (today there are 4,800 DQs globally). *The New York World's Fair* was in its second and final year, and one of the features was a new entertainment medium called television. While it was something fascinating, it would be several years before this new medium would begin to have any impact. It did show a few sports events locally in 1940, but many predicted it would never replace radio. It was just nothing more than a passing fad. It would be too expensive for anyone to own and have in their home. Little did anyone know then just what a profound effect this "fad" would have on the country, the world, the future and how we would live and learn in so many ways.

Meanwhile on the big band/swing front several changes were taking place. While it was still king, the wild hysteria it had caused early on settled into a more relaxed, but always building fandom among people of every age. They were still packing venues, big band radio shows were making advertisers happy, record sales and sheet music sales were still at the top. It was another year that would see a few more new bands hit the scene quick to capture an audience bringing even more styles to the dancers. There was **Eddy Howard**, **Orin Tucker**, **Jimmy Dorsey** returned with a new band and two popular singers, **Bob Eberly** and **Helen O'Connell**. **Harry James** was doing very well thanks in part to his boy singer, **Frank Sinatra** who had become a very big bobby sox favorite with the females. There was also another band out of South Dakota, of all places, making some regional headlines, playing to full ballrooms in the Midwest.

The band was somewhat on the sweet side, but had a lot of very good swing numbers that were very danceable and popular with their fan base. However, this band would never achieve any national fame during the big band/swing era. That success and popularity would come sometime later in the 1950's when they would become one of the most popular shows on TV for many years after. The band we refer to was the **Lawrence Welk Orchestra**.

While no one had a crystal ball to foresee the future, many of the bands and the arrangers were adding patriotic songs to their music library. Part of it was because of the peace time draft now in place and felt like the right thing to do. Apparently they were right, because the band's fans and followers enjoyed these songs, even though some were hard to dance to. Many young musicians were giving up their band suits for army khakis or Navy blue as they enlisted in the service. Just about every band working was being affected to some degree as they scrambled to find replacement musicians who could not only play the music but able to read charts, some that were very intricate. Overall, some 16,000,000 men had signed up for the draft. By the end of 1940, over 75,000 had actually gone on active duty in various branches of the military. The shortened supply of experienced musicians to fill the gaps prompted bandleader *Ozzie Nelson* to write a humorous but prolific song titled *"We're Looking for an Alto Man Who Doubles on Clarinet and Wears a Size 37 suit."* Despite some of the changes, the bands were still doing very well. Record and sheet music sales were still at high levels, audiences for the big band radio shows were still strong, and crowds were still huge at restaurants, ballrooms, and clubs to see the many different bands in person.

Once again in 1940, it would be *Glenn Miller* ruling the charts and lead the way with 11 Top 10 songs, four being #1. Miller was still being courted by Hollywood but again made it clear he was not interested in what they wanted from him. He did not want his band, with their popularity, to just be a

one scene setup playing a song. He wanted the band and himself to be a part of the story and for the band to have an actual role in a film. So without that, and not really needing Hollywood anyway, Miller again turned them down. While some thought he was asking for way too much, Glenn knew the day would come when Hollywood would give him what he wanted. Also hitting the charts that year with great songs, big record sales and packed personal appearances were **Goodman**, **Dorsey**, **Shaw**, **Barnet**, **Clinton** and others. There was one new band that really came on strong and that was the **Les Brown Orchestra**. His brand of swing caught on very quick with dancers and his very polished sound on slow, romantic ballads was hit with both the young and older generation. But it was the appearance of his new, 17-year old blonde singer who, with her silky voice, became a very popular attraction. Her given name was Doris Kappelhoff. Brown quickly changed it to **Doris Day**. Of course, not only would Ms. Day become one of the era's top band vocalists, but after the big bands faded, had a very long and very successful solo recording career and also a major movie career for many years after. One small side note, today at age 92, Ms. Day is, to our knowledge and research, the only surviving member left from the big band and swing era.

While big band/swing music was the most popular music of the day, it had settled into a very comfortable groove. On any given night, with your favorite band playing either on radio, on record, or in person you could cut a rug with the jitterbug or hold your lady close dancing to the romantic ballads. There were the picturesque places to go like **Glen Island Casino**, **The Meadowbrook**, **Elitch Gardens** and it wasn't uncommon for engagements or marriage proposals to take place at these establishments with the big bands becoming the musical backdrop for these surprise announcements. In 1940, when it came to the weekend, places were packed to the rafters. The mix of people and ages showed another change as it was now an age group that pretty much went 18 to 80, all getting along and enjoying a night out with the best music on the planet supplied by the best bands in the land. By the final month of 1940 *Miller*, *Dorsey* and *Goodman* led the record charts scoring almost three dozen hits among them in the Top Ten lists. A number of the other bands also made the Top Ten and number ones as well but none came close to what those three had done. Most of all it continued to solidify the popularity of all of the bands as well as the debut of more new bands from coast to coast. The future looked and felt very bright indeed as the country was about to enter another exciting new year filled with a lot of promise, but also one major surprise.

CHAPTER 3

1941 – 1945

THE WAR YEARS & THE BIG BANDS

The year *1941* began on a high note for the country. The work force continued to grow, with fewer people on unemployment as new projects of every description were underway everywhere across the country. There were homes to skyscrapers, hotels to highways and autos, ships and planes being built everywhere. Families were enjoying time together, kids were kids enjoying school and other activities, and there was plenty of entertainment to keep everyone happy. In addition to sports, there were some great movies like in *"The Bank Dick"*, starring comedian W.C. Fields. *Orson Welles*, who scared the living daylights out of everyone in 1938 with his *"War of the Worlds"* radio broadcast, starring in *"Citizen Kane"*. Also from Hollywood in 1941 were *How Green Was My Valley*, *The Maltese Falcon*, and *Sergeant York*. On radio, *Hope*, *Benny*, *Allen*, and *Edgar Bergen* were still big, but there was also Gang Busters, Superman, Kate Smith, Grand Central Station and a brand new show from Chicago, Don McNeil's *Breakfast Club*. People were now paying closer attention to the news from abroad and reports coming from Washington and overseas from the radio news voices. The most listened to, as we had mentioned earlier, were **Gabriel Heatter**, **Lowell Thomas** and **H.V. Kaltenborn**. There was also a young reporter for CBS, **Edward R. Murrow** who was keeping the American public up on all that was taking place in Europe, Great Britain and its effect on the entire world. Murrow was closely listened to because he was broadcasting his reports live every day or night right from the battle scarred scenes in Europe and Great Britain. His reports were blunt, up front and caught the attention of everyone.

On the home front, workers were kept busy in the factories and plants, not only building and assembling products for home use, but also supplies for our allies as well as our own growing military. With the peacetime draft, more young men continued to sign up and join. In a 2-year period, the entire U.S. military had tripled in size. It was also in 1941 that the **USO** would be formed so that servicemen would have places to go while they were away from home and family. FDR continued to calm the American public, saying we would remain neutral with what was taking place across the Atlantic. However, by now there was no denying the country could feel the swirling forces of war across the Atlantic. The big question remained whether those winds of war in Europe would ever come upon our shores. In spite of what some may

have thought, our military growth and with more products for the military being produced, there was still a positive feeling as the American people continued to have an abiding faith in FDR and continue to do their patriotic best to help our allies while still looking ahead to this country's own future and protection. There was a growing silent fear of a clear and present danger, but it was 8,000 miles away and was nothing to really worry about. The U.S. would be just fine and escape the horrors that were taking place in other parts of the world. At the same time, there was also little or no concern about what was going on over 10,000 miles away to our west.

Everything was as normal as one could expect. People went on vacations, spent time with family, church on Sundays, the movies, ballgames and restaurants. Couples, both young and old, made dancing to the bands at various ballrooms and clubs a big part of their spare time. Young people looked forward to the school year, getting diplomas, going on to college, and going to dances on the weekends. The unemployment numbers continued to drop; people were making a decent wage for the time and were actually able to save a little for a rainy day. The peacetime draft did have an effect, not only on the bands, but in the private sector as well. A lot of young men decided to enlist in the military after graduating high school rather than get a job or go to college. The bands were able to find some excellent replacements and continue the tours, radio shows, recordings and personal appearances without missing a beat. In 1941, there was no slowdown in record and sheet music sales. The theaters and ballrooms were doing solid business and radio shows were still doing well. Unfortunately one problem arose musically due to a ban by ASCAP, the music organization that handles royalties for writers and publishers. Because of the popularity of the bands and radio shows ASCAP wanted a bigger slice of the royalties so they banned any song that was published by ASCAP to be performed on the radio. This forced the bands to begin playing songs in the "public domain". This meant creating arrangements for old semi classical, classical and folk songs, etc. that no longer had any copyright. This change actually worked for some of the bands when they added these songs with either a slow romantic beat or a swing beat to them. The ban didn't hurt as much as it could have and also gave the bands something new to add to their music libraries. Some of these "new" songs even became top chart hits for a few. There was **Les Brown's "Bizet Has His Day"**, **Glenn Miller's '"Rhapsody in Blue"** and **"Song of the Volga Boatmen"**, **Larry Clinton's "Our Love"** and **Artie Shaw's "La Paloma"**, among the songs that became both danceable and popular hits. The ban only pertained to what songs the bands played on radio, not on recordings and would only last into October of '41. This short ban would help create another music organization, BMI, who offered a bit more leniency to the radio situation.

Even with the ban for a little more than 6 months, it didn't slow things down as the bands traveled all over the country doing personal appearances, radio shows, were in the recording studio and maintained their popularity. Once again though, and thanks in a big part to **Glenn Miller**, the entire body of big band music had been elevated again both in appearances and on recordings. It was in 1941 that Miller finally got what he wanted from Hollywood as well. The band headed west to make their first major film, **"Sun Valley Serenade"** starring **Sonja Henie**, **John Payne** and **Lynn Bari**. Payne played the role of Miller's pianist, Bari was his love interest and the girl singer in the band. It also co-starred a young **Milton Berle** who played Glenn's manager. The band not only played their musical numbers but some, including Miller, had actual acting roles in the film.

No surprise it would be an Oscar nominee for music that year. Needless to say, the movie was also a smash hit at the box office. As the year moved on several new bands came on

the scene, **Teddy Powell**, **Jack Teagarden**, **Stan Kenton**, **Shep Fields** (who had revised much of his library to become a more swingy band), **Frankie Carle**, **Spike Jones** and **Freddy Slack** were among those making their debuts in 1941. In other areas that year there was the introduction of sharp new cars from Detroit. (Check out the photo of that classy '41 Pontiac). There was a new product that would become very big years later called Teflon. Two brand new breakfast cereals came on the market, Cheerios and Rice Krispies. Baseball fans kept up with two milestones, Joe DiMaggio's '56 game-hitting streak and Ted Williams quest to hit .400 (he would wind up hitting .406). A new appliance for the kitchen, the garbage disposal, was introduced. In Corbin, Kentucky a family restaurant called **Saunders' Homemade Chicken** would open for business and years later would become better known as **Kentucky Fried Chicken**. It was also a year where people were really now becoming much more concerned with what was taking place in Great Britain and Europe. Our factories and plants stepped up production to help our allies and to build up our growing military. FDR once again continued to tell the American public we were remaining neutral only supplying our allies with materials and equipment. But while there was a growing doubt we could stay neutral, it was the unwavering faith in FDR that caused them not to worry much and hope everything would come to a peaceful end across the Atlantic. By the time Thanksgiving 1941 came, everyone was in a festive mood, enjoyed the parades, the big football games and seeing family and friends on Turkey Day. We had many things to be thankful for on that day and thoughts were now on the coming of Christmas, another great year and bright future. For just about everyone 1941 had been an extremely good year in so many ways.

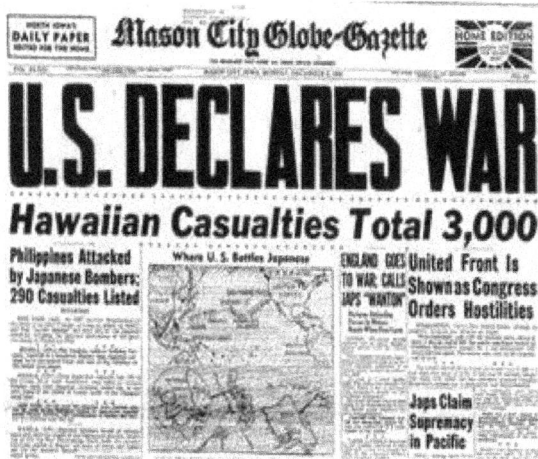

Then suddenly came that devastating morning December 7, 1941. Every ounce of positive energy America had now turned to anger and horror as word came on the radio the Japanese had made a sneak air attack on Pearl Harbor, bombing and sinking our ships, damaging our planes, leaving many dead and wounded. FDR came on the radio at about 4 p.m. EST (there is a 6-hour time difference between Hawaii and Washington, D.C.) and would deliver his now famous "Dec. 7, 1941, a day that will live in infamy" speech about what had taken place at Pearl and then officially declaring war against the Empire of Japan. Within days the United States would also declare war against Germany and Italy. Suddenly the country was smack dab in the middle of a world war. A war that was about to change this country and the world we live in forever. Never again would anything ever be the same throughout the entire world.

Suddenly, all of the prosperity, good feelings, and excitement about the future were put on hold. No one knew for how long this war would last or what the future might hold for everyone now. The winds of war from the west and now from the east were intensely very real. No longer was it just radio reports or newsreel films. Reality was staring us in the face. Men of all ages flocked to the nearest recruiting centers to enlist and join the military. Those who were turned down because of age or a medical problem would, for the most part, do their patriotic best by going to work in many of the shipyards or the factories. In a matter of days and weeks just about every factory, mill or plant throughout the country ceased the normal operations of what they were producing and now turning all their efforts to military hardware, weapons, armament, supplies, vehicles, aircraft and more. Families coast to coast saw fathers, sons, uncles, nephews, and brothers shipping out to various bases for

Photo # NH 98597 USS Philip and USS Renshaw ready for launching, at Kearny, N.J., 13 October 1942

basic training before being sent to various parts of the world to fight our enemies. It was an extremely emotional time for families in Everytown, U.S.A. While this country had come together before in times of trouble, this time they did it as never before. The people banded together with scrap drives, bond drives, volunteering at USOs and other functions like Civil Defense. People began to grow victory gardens and doing anything and everything they could to help the war effort at home. I was just 6 years old, but remember Dec. 7, 1941 in the minutest detail as if were yesterday. I remember exactly what I was doing and what my folks were doing when that announcement came on the radio. I remember going with my mother on scrap drives and being with her when she volunteered at the church and helping plant our Victory garden. My father broke up his band a short time later and put away his saxophones, exchanging them for riveting tools and going to work at the shipyards in Jersey City. Like me, anyone who grew up during that time, remembers vividly what that infamous day was like and the weeks, months and years that would follow until it came to an end.

FDR made it very clear that he did not want the country to shut down because diversions would be needed for the people. He told Hollywood, radio and the big bands to keep producing movies and music. He told baseball and football, even with the loss of players to keep going and give people what they would need after working long hours in factories, plants and the shipyards.

It was a tall order considering the number of professional athletes and movie stars that were now going into the military. Bandleaders **Artie Shaw**, **Eddy Duchin**, **Ted Weems**, **Clyde McCoy** were among those who shut their bands down and joined the service. **Glenn Miller** wanted to join the Army and sent letters off to volunteer, but it would be the following year before Miller would leave the bandstand. In Hollywood stars like **Clark Gable**, **Charlton Heston**, **David Niven**, **George C. Scott**, **Tyrone Power**, **Gene Kelly**, **Henry Fonda**, **Ernest Borgnine**, **Jimmy Stewart** were among those off to war. In baseball some of the big

names who traded bats and balls for machine guns and aircraft were **Ted Williams**, **Bob Feller**, **Bill Dickey**, **Enos Slaughter**, **Warren Spahn**, **Hank Greenberg**, **Joe DiMaggio**, **Stan Musial**, **Ralph Kiner**. In all, 400 major league players that would see military service at some time during World War II. It was also at this time **Bob Hope** would begin his **USO**

tours to entertain the troops overseas, something Hope would continue to do unselfishly for the next 50 years.

Now, with the country fully immersed in a world war with Germany, Italy and Japan, factories, plants and shipyards worked round the clock, seven days a week to get products, supplies, airplanes and ships and whatever else was needed done in record time. It is amazing to look back at that time and to realize without all the technology of today, jobs that normally would have taken months were done in weeks. It was an incredible production pace by the American work force that never let up. It was a time when factories and plants didn't care if you were male or female, if you could do the job required you were hired. It was a very hectic and stressful pace for everyone involved, but with time of the essence, the American work force went nonstop. Everyone had a huge sense of patriotism and American pride and would do whatever needed to be done in any way they could to support the war effort from home. When there was some free time everyone needed a break from the pressure and emotion of what the country was going through. For that, they would turn to radio, go to a movie, a ballgame and dance to the music of the big bands. Unfortunately a couple of incidents would take place during the worst time possible. These happenings would only serve to hasten what would be the beginning of the downfall of the big band/swing era.

In *1942*, the big bands had to curtail a number of appearances because of gas rationing, rationing on tires and many other goods because the war effort obviously took precedence. There was rationing on just about everything but the people, though inconvenient, knew it had to be done. So ration books became a way of life for the American family. We were in a full-fledged war in two different parts of the world and our entire, and still growing, military was literally all around the globe fighting to bring peace to the world. Not only had our military grown by huge numbers, but the Army and Air Force had now become a major factor as fighter planes and bombers were being built and put into action in record time. Whatever it was our military needed, as well as our allies, the factories, plants, mills, and other businesses in the marketplace would provide it efficiently and quickly. It was amazing to see the number of ships built and launched from various shipyards around the country, and the massive numbers of planes being ferried from the factories to air bases both in the U.S. and abroad.

The bands did continue to play and entertain, but due to rationing could only travel short distances from where they were based. This meant staying at a place for a week or two to save on gas, tires, etc. So bands who were based out of New York rarely traveled more than 200 miles, same with bands in the Midwest and on the West Coast. But it did not diminish the public's need for the entertainment they provided in a very emotional time. Radio continued to be a very big plus, but record sales suffered a big drop as many of the materials used to make records were now wartime necessities. It was the same with sheet music; production was cut with paper needed for much more important projects. During 1942 and based on the success of the first film, *Glenn Miller* and his orchestra went to Hollywood to film their second movie, titled *"Orchestra Wives"*. In this one, **George Montgomery** starred as Glenn's trumpet player and **Cesar Romero** as Miller's piano player with **Ann Rutherford** and **Lyn Bari** as the love interests. Bari would also again play the girl singer in the band (her singing was done by **Pat Friday**). Also in the film playing Miller's bass player was a young, little-known Jackie Gleason. Between the great Miller music, which was nominated for an Oscar, and the fun love story it was a perfect film for people to take their minds off war, rationing and jobs for a few hours. Glenn had two more films in the works but they were put on hold. After the band completed work on *"Orchestra Wives"* they made one more final personal appearance. It took place at the **Capitol Theater** in Passaic, New Jersey to a standing room-only crowd. Glenn then shut the band down and would enter the Army Air Force.

To keep the morale up of our military a number of the big bands **Goodman**, **Dorsey**, **Ellington**, **Herman**, **James**, **Barnet**, **Basie**, **Clinton**, and others made it a point to play at various military bases around the country. They were a welcome addition for the troops before they shipped out to the Far East or Europe and the battles of war. The big band era had fought through a strike in 1941 over royalties with the radio networks and when all was said and done everything had been worked out to the satisfaction of all involved. Now, a year later and at a time when the music of the big bands was of major importance to everyone as a morale builder, one man set out to end that. **James C. Petrillo**, the head of the AFM (American Federation of Musicians) didn't care about morale or what was best for the people at the time.

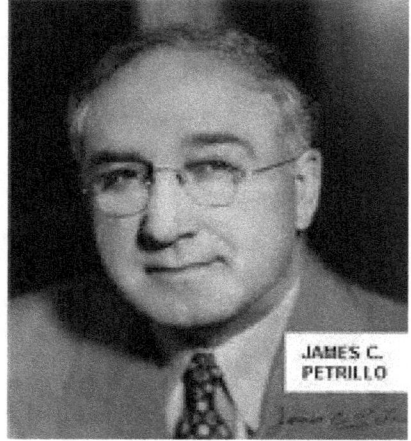

JAMES C. PETRILLO

Instead, he called for a ban on all recordings by the bands unless they were given more royalty money. Because of their popularity, there was no question they did deserve more, but the country was at war and this strike was not wanted or needed. Many of the top bandleaders and musicians begged Petrillo to wait until the war ended and deal with it then, but Petrillo stuck to his ban and would not relent. Even several politicians asked him to hold off and he wouldn't budge. At first, it really didn't hurt because there was a big backlog of recordings previously done, not yet released that would not be affected by the ban. But as the latter part of 1942 came along, between the rationing of materials and the ban, it opened the door for vocalists' recordings. So singers like **Frank Sinatra**, **Perry Como**, **Vaughn Monroe**, **Lena Horne**, **Ella Fitzgerald**, **Bing Crosby**, **Peggy Lee**, **Dinah Shore**, and others began recording songs and also using voices in the background to sound like

instruments or add harmonies much like **Ray Coniff** would do in the '60's and '70's. The **Frank Sinatra** pandemonium had been sweeping the country not only with **Harry James**, but after he moved over to the **Tommy Dorsey Orchestra** before going out on his own. He was selling out shows and appearances everywhere and his CBS radio show **"Reflections"** had become a runaway hit on the airwaves. The ban on recordings would last until late 1943, almost one full year, but the damage had been done and served, unknowingly, as a premature death knell for the big bands as the vocalists had now become the popular stars.

In **1943**, it was now Major **Glenn Miller** in the Army Air Corps, and he was assigned to Maxwell AFB in Alabama to conduct the marching band at the base, but Miller had other ideas. He rubbed a lot of shoulders the wrong way, especially when he took a song like **"St. Louis Blues"** and turned it into a combination of jazz, swing, and marching music. Except for a few higher-ups, most everyone in the command felt that Miller was out of line. He also did some radio shows for the military, but persisted in getting the higher ups to listen to what he really wanted to do and felt would work best not only for him, but for the military, the troops, the allies and especially the morale. What he fought for and finally got was to get as many of his old musicians assigned to him, reform his band and add some good military musicians and then tour bases in England and elsewhere. He felt it was essential to give the troops something from home they were missing and needed while they were fighting a war. Finally with the help of a couple of high ranking Generals, Major Glenn Miller got the band he wanted and headed for England to begin what

would turn into hundreds of appearances in front of U.S., British, and allied troops in some of the most dangerous places. For the hour or so they played, sometimes as sirens went off, or having to scramble for cover, it made everything seem right. After the war, many veterans said that being able to see and hear Glenn Miller and his band play during the war was the best morale builder they could have had at the time.

During this period while some places like the **Meadowbrook**, **Glen Island Casino**, **Elitch Gardens**, and **Palomar** along with some others stayed open and did, it just wasn't the same. Between the war, bands shutting down, losing members to the military, restrictions on travel and the ill-timed recording strike a lot of the luster was now being lost. Radio still helped, but even that was beginning to feel the pinch as record sales and commercial advertisers saw a big drop in revenue. In addition, the bands were now playing more patriotic songs, and while it was done for obvious reasons, most of those songs were not danceable. There were just too many things that had begun to happen after Petrillo called for the recording ban that slowly began the demise of the era. Even with continued pleading from record labels, band leaders and even various civic leaders, Petrillo refused to back down on his demands. While Petrillo's egotistical stubbornness was a major cause of the shift in the big band's popularity, it wasn't the only reason. There was one other incident that would take place that really delivered a final crushing blow. We will get into that a little further on.

At home, people continued to take part in scrap drives, bond drives, dealing with rationing of just about everything in their daily lives. Victory gardens were still being grown in just about every home that had a back yard. There were the civil defense and air raid tests, and the volunteers

who helped. There were even blackouts and curfews imposed in many towns, as people prepared and worried just how close to our shores the Germans and Japanese might actually come. There were men and women working side by side, making gun parts and airplane parts, assembling bombers and building war ships. They worked at a feverish pitch around the clock continuing to turn out everything the military needed in record breaking time. It was a time when *"Rosie the Riveter"* became famous in song because of so many women working in these plants and factories. There was very little resistance when women started working at various jobs. We were at war and every able-bodied person was needed. Right from the start women proved how efficient they were with tools and being able to keep up the pace. The simple fact is without women joining the work force during the war much of the production would not have been accomplished in the record time that it was. As I mentioned before, my father had broken up his band right after a New Year's Eve engagement. He went to work at the Jersey City shipyards where they were building destroyers for the Navy. He would stay with the shipyards through 1946, but never again assembled his big band. He sensed the change and used small four and five piece groups he'd assemble for occasional club or dance engagements.

In *1943*, people still had their diversions to get their mind off the grueling work schedules and the pressures of war. When it came to going to the local movie house among the big pictures they enjoyed were *Casablanca, The Ox-Bow Incident, Phantom of the Opera, My Friend Flicka*, and *Song of Bernadette*. The radio gave folks *The Judy Canova Show, Groucho Marx, Jack Benny, Information Please*, Nick Carter Master Detective, *Tom Brenneman's Breakfast In Hollywood* and many others along with the daily

newscasts. They still had sporting events to go to get their minds off war troubles for a few hours, including something new. P.K. Wrigley and Branch Rickey formed the **AAGPBL** (All-American Girls Professional Baseball League). There were 6 teams in the league in the Midwest and they played in regular minor league ballparks using the same rules as the men. It took a while to gather a fan base but once it did these talented ladies filled the ballparks and the league would last until 1954. But for the war years this new league had served its purpose giving people another entertainment diversion. In 1992, Hollywood released a biographic film about the AAGPBL called *A League of Their Own* that starred *Geena Davis* and *Tom Hanks*. Besides radio, movies and sports there were still some new additions that came along in 1943. A brand new magazine called *Seventeen* made its debut. Chicago got its first subway and people got their first taste of Chicago-styled pizza. Housewives liked the new Uncle Ben's Converted Rice, and the military had a new building in D.C. called the Pentagon. While all this was taking place, there would be one very ugly incident to happen and would leave a big black mark on the country for a long, long time, but it was also a sign of the times people lived in back then.

While there were no problems anywhere else in the country when it came to jobs, in Detroit it was a different story. Here, the U.S. was in the middle of world war, doing its very best to get products, munitions, equipment, etc. to our troops, with men injured and killed in every war theater and racism and bigotry would raise its ugly head. The whites objected very strongly to blacks getting jobs at defense-related positions in factories and plants. This prejudice would escalate so bad that it turned into the *Detroit Riots* in June of 1943. It became a very ugly scene at a time when every able-bodied

person, regardless of color, was needed to work and help in the war effort. In these ensuing riots, 29 people were killed and hundreds more were injured, many critically. This deplorable and devastating incident slowed down production at a number of defense plants as those

wounded could not return to work right away. It would force the closing of schools, nighttime curfews, looting and result in hundreds of arrests. It got so bad and out of control, the Federal troops were finally called in to help the Detroit police restore order. While it was denounced by FDR and the administration, it was the perfect propaganda for Hitler to use against the U.S. This riot left an embarrassing mark on the rest of the country. What made this even more nonsensical was the fact that we had black units fighting in Europe and the South Pacific. Eisenhower would finally put an end to discrimination in the Army where black and white would fight together. There was the all-black flying unit, the Tuskegee Airmen, as they were called, who were celebrated by their white superiors and fellow airmen for the extraordinary job they were doing as escorts for the squadrons of B-17's during bombing raids over Germany. This amazing and selfless group of black pilots would be honored for their service many years later. The Detroit incident would embarrass every American to the core, as it was the only time something like this would take place during the war years. What would happen after the war regarding discrimination and a fight for civil rights would be another ugly story.

We mentioned earlier in this segment about *"Rosie the Riveter"* and how women became such an important part of the war effort at home. There were also women who both signed up for, as well as volunteered, as nurses to help take care of our wounded and injured both here at

home and abroad. Many nurses landed in Germany, France, and Great Britain and gave of themselves to treat the wounded. There was also another group of dedicated women whose contribution to WW II has gone mainly forgotten and without any fanfare, or worthy honor or tribute for their service. Those were the hundreds of brave women who flew and ferried aircraft from the factories to military bases in the states as well as Europe. It would lead to the formation of the WASPs, the women's Air Force unit, just as there would be the WACs for the Army and WAVES for the Navy. There has never been any question how American women played very important and vital part in the war effort as did the blacks, native Americans, and those thousands of mixed heritages. Without the entire nation coming together as one, it would have been an even tougher period to get things done the way they were. Other than the embarrassing mess in Detroit, no company cared about skin color or heritage; they only wanted one thing from their workers—100% dedication to their job and country in helping to win the war by their service at home. That is another reason why what took place will always be remembered and be a very embarrassing mark on the city of Detroit at a time when every man and woman's contribution to the war effort was essential and working together as one, as real true Americans have always done.

The U.S. entered *1944* with the Detroit incident behind and productivity going at a record-breaking pace. On the plus side, there were some strong signs, at least in the European theater, that missions were taking a turn for the better. Hitler and the Nazis were close to being on the verge of collapse as the U.S. and allied troops kept beating them at every battle and every turn. A total collapse from the Germans could be felt as well as surrender, it now just a matter of time. In the Pacific, change was slowly moving in our favor, but that battle still had a long way to go as the Japanese Navy and Air Force were relentless. All the positives were there and back home everyone was hoping and praying the end was close at hand. This didn't mean any slowdown as planes, ships, tanks, etc. continued to be built and deployed to our troops. All of the defense plants were still going 24/7 and rationing was still in full effect. There were still Civil Defense and Air Raid tests being

done just in case. Now in his unprecedented 4th term as president, FDR, in his always-confident tone, assured the public victory was not far off. On June 6, 1944, a date which would become famously known as **D-Day**, the landing on Normandy would signal the eventual end of the war in Europe. In the Pacific, the Navy and Marines had been fighting fierce battles with the Japanese. The time had now come for the Army Air Force to get more involved. It would be this next step that would begin to signal the end of the war in the Pacific, but the Japanese were not going to go easily. With Tokyo the main target, dozens of B-25 Mitchell bombers took off from carriers in the Sea of Japan and made successful bombing raids on Japan's capitol city. Those bombing missions would only serve as a warning to the Japanese of what was yet to come and

soon bring them to final surrender and an end to the war.

As for the entertainment picture in 1944, to help people take their minds off all of war news, radio provided enjoyment with a lot of new shows like **Dragnet**, **Gunsmoke**, **Buelah**, **Dr. Keen Tracer of Lost Persons**, and **The Adventures of Ozzie and Harriet**, as well as the old

standbys. Naturally, as it had been throughout the war, many programs would be interrupted with news bulletins to keep the people up to date. On June 6, D-Day, just about all regular radio programming was suspended as the country got up to date reports on the landing at Normandy. The big band radio shows had now dwindled down to only two or three. Radio shows were now featuring the singers including **Frank Sinatra**, **Bing Crosby**, **The Andrews Sisters**, **Dinah Shore** and a musical show that enjoyed a very long life in both radio and later television, **Your Hit Parade**. Baseball fans watched history in the making when the St. Louis Browns, one of the worst teams in baseball, went to the World Series to play their in-city rival, the St. Louis Cardinals, only to lose. The women's league, the AAGPBL, was packing them in at stadiums throughout the Midwest. Another sport which began back in the early '30's was also starting to take hold around the country with its fast paced rough, tough action with both men and women competing, the **Roller Derby**. It would go on to become a major hit in the '50's on TV. When it came to the movies, among the films people enjoyed were **Meet Me in St. Louis**, **Thirty Seconds Over Tokyo**, **Double Indemnity**, and **National Velvet** which introduced moviegoers to a very young **Elizabeth Taylor**. It was also the year **Batman and Robin** made a debut in the newspaper comics, along with **Blondie and Dagwood**. Rationing, blackouts, travel restrictions, and curfews were still in order. Ration coins came along in 1944 that allowed retailers to give change back for food bought with ration stamps. However, a cut back began and certain foods and products were no longer being rationed. While there seemed to be a bright light at the end of the tunnel, the war had a way to go before it was time to celebrate. There were still the Victory gardens and bond drives being done. Now, in addition to American flags being displayed everywhere, there was now a display of gold and silver banners hanging in the windows of many homes throughout the land indicating loved ones killed or injured in action. The war plodded on throughout Europe as the U.S. and its allies went about putting the final nails into the coffin of Hitler's Nazi regime. In the Pacific the air, sea and land battles raged on as the U.S. continued its heavy and unrelenting assault on the Japanese. As one Japanese

Admiral in the Imperial Navy had remarked back in 1942, the Japanese Empire had awakened a sleeping giant and would now pay the price. That price would be a very, very expensive one and begin being paid starting in February of 1945.

Just as the war and the recording strike combined to begin the big band era's downslide, there was another incident that came along and one more reason that would cause the real start of the big band era's downfall It was a real ill-timed move. Somehow, both Congress and the Senate voted to approve a 30% excise tax on any ballrooms, clubs, or restaurants that provided dancing to live music. This immediately caused many of the top ballrooms to suddenly close and soon go out of business. It now meant less places for the bands to play and for the people to see them. Many of the restaurants changed formats eliminating music. As if that weren't enough for the bands, the clubs, ballrooms and the fans to handle, one more jarring piece of news unexpectedly came along and would have a profound impact on the

coming death of the big band era. It was so out of the ordinary that no one could have predicted something like this could happen, even in war time. But this shocking event would be felt throughout the entire world and change the face of music forever.

By 1944, Major Glenn Miller had gotten his band together, added some musicians, and was doing all kinds of tours of military bases all over the UK and Europe. He was based in Great Britain, where he occasionally did a radio broadcast back home, but mainly entertained the troops overseas amid bombing raids, sirens going off and generally not the best of conditions. However, his music was so important that while some appearances would get cut short, not one was ever cancelled. The band was scheduled to go to Paris for a couple of shows and to broadcast a special Christmas show that would be heard both in Europe and throughout the United States. It was also the first time the Miller band would have a complete string section added to it to give the band a fuller, richer sound, something Miller had wanted to experiment with and maybe use after the war. He sent the band ahead to Paris to rehearse while he finished up some military business in England and would join the band a couple of days later in Paris. The radio show and engagements in Paris were also going to be the last performances of the band as Miller was scheduled to be discharged in January 1945 and resume civilian life. He already had begun working on plans for the band to make one last tour of the U.S., do one more film that had been put on hold. He had offers from Hollywood to write and arrange music for several studios and also had thoughts of starting his own publishing and management firm. No question Glenn Miller had his eye on the future and all he wanted to accomplish. Unfortunately, those dreams would never be realized because on that fateful December day the big band era, for all intents and purposes, would pretty much come to a close. It would be the day the music died, just as it would 15 years later in a snow-covered Iowa cornfield.

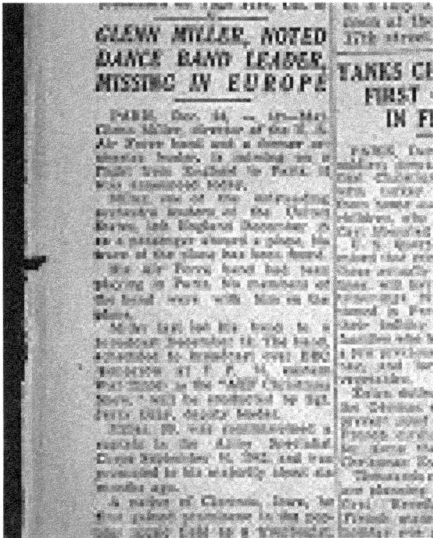

On December 15, Miller and his pilot took off in a small Norseman recon plane in cold and damp weather that was also hindered by a heavy shroud of fog that enveloped the area as they headed for their Paris destination. Somewhere over the English Channel, the plane was lost and both the plane and bodies have never been recovered. All communications with the plane were lost via radio and radar. Many attempts right up until this day have been made by various historical groups and foundations to locate the plane and bodies, but with no success. It has long been suspected because the Norseman it had no de-icing equipment, which might have been a main cause of the plane going down. When word reached Paris about what had taken place, shock would be an understatement as to how band members and those close to Miller reacted. However, the band persevered, pulled itself together, and went on with the Christmas radio shows as scheduled. Many have said, including those who were in the band then, that it was the greatest performance the **Glenn Miller Orchestra**, civilian or military, had ever given. Many of the musicians said it was tough to play through the tears and emotions as they felt Miller's presence that day. For pianist Chummy McGregor, Miller's friend since childhood, it was an especially tough time to play the arrangements through the tears. Amid all the talk of war on the radio, the reports of Miller's passing sent shockwaves throughout the country and the entire music and film industry, as well as the White House. With all the losses of lives of fathers, uncles, brothers, sisters, cousins, close friends, etc., the loss of Glenn Miller, to millions, was like losing a family member. Miller's impact on the American way of life went far beyond the bandstand. Even the stuffy *New York Times* finally admitted that they were wrong, doing a glowing tribute to Miller upon his passing.

With the success of D-Day and subsequent battles all over Europe, it was now only a matter of time before the Germans would surrender and the war in Europe would finally come to an end at the cost of countless lives. However, there was still a lot to be done to make sure the reign of terror from Hitler would never again take place. The bombings and ground assaults continued as the Germans kept getting pushed back. Knowing defeat was at hand, Hitler committed suicide in an underground bunker, and the Nazi regime quickly fell like a house of cards. It was the same in the Pacific. The bombings of Tokyo had sent a clear message to the Japanese empire, but they kept fighting in the air, on the ground and at sea refusing to give up. It would take something massive to finally put an end to the war with Japan, and that something was just about ready to be unveiled.

CHAPTER 4

1945 – 1947

POST WAR TIMES BRING A BIG CHANGE

As 1945 came into view, there was a positive sense that the end of the war was on the horizon. At the same time the music world, and fans, were still reeling from the loss of Glenn Miller. Some of the bandleaders kept the home fires burning, like **Tommy Dorsey**, **Benny Goodman**, **Russ Morgan**, **Artie Shaw**, **Kay Kyser**, **Les Brown**, **Count Basie**, and a few others continued to play at clubs, on radio, and appear at the dwindling number of ballrooms. In a tribute to Miller, some of the bands added their versions of previous Glenn Miller hits to their libraries. A few band leaders had returned from their military service and began to reform their bands. The hope was with the end of the war in sight, the bands and swing music could get back to where it had been prior to the war and recapture that glory.

It was a very tall order because so much had changed. Even the most optimistic people in the music industry were very skeptical the past would be brought back with so many changes taking place. The two that hurt the industry the most, as far as bands went, was the recording strike by Petrillo and then the excise tax on clubs and ballrooms by the government. Then add in many other changes in life in general and it was now a totally different time from a few years ago. In April 1945, the country suffered a major tragedy with the passing of President *Franklin Delano Roosevelt*, who had been in ill health for some time, but still ran the country like a finely-tuned engine. FDR had served as president since 1932 and oversaw the rise from the Depression, then getting us through the war while keeping the American spirit high. It was a shame, after all he had accomplished over the years, that FDR wouldn't live to see surrender and peace finally come. His funeral in Washington and the procession were unlike anything ever seen for any U.S. President. After the procession and memorial in Washington, FDR's body went by special train through towns big and small all over the country, as millions lined the tracks along the route to pay their respects to a man who had led this country for 14 years. FDR's Vice President, *Harry S. Truman*, stepped right in and didn't miss a beat. Truman had been by FDR's side and well aware of what the plans had been to put an end to the war. Truman immediately directed the Army and Air Force to finish the job in Europe allowing them carte blanche to do whatever was needed, and they accomplished it in quick order. The Germans surrendered unconditionally on May 8, 1945. It was VE Day back in the states as the war in Europe was over and now the liberation began. The

celebrating that took place back in the U.S. was like New Year's Eve wherever you went. Truman, while glad to see one phase of the war ended, was quick to warn the people that while celebrating this victory, there was still the Japanese to deal with, and our job was not yet completed to end this war and restore peace. Now it was time to put the plan that had been designed and approved by the administration into full effect. This plan would bring the Japanese to total surrender and bring a new weapon of warfare into the picture.

By now production of materials for the military was still a priority, but many plants and factories were slowly getting back to their normal production of other goods. A lot of the rationing had been ended by President Truman. While the work force was now a mix of doing wartime jobs and regular jobs, people had developed a better sense of peace and enjoyed time off going to the movies, ballgames and listening to their favorite radio shows. Speaking of radio, there was also something new taking place on the airwaves. In some of the major cities like New York, Chicago, and Los Angeles, you could tune in your radio and listen to "disc jockeys", who played recordings on the air and would develop personalities. One of the most popular back then, and for years after, was **Martin Block** on WNEW in New York City and his **"Make Believe Ballroom"** show that garnered a huge audience and paved the way for more disc jockeys and record shows. Block actually began doing this back in the early '30's, but its zenith began to climb in the mid '40's and really hit its peak in the '50's, '60's and '70's. As disc jockeys became more popular, the "personality" format would completely change the face of radio from what it had been since the 1920's. Like everything else that was undergoing change by now, so would radio. Still, with all these changes taking place there, was one more serious problem to be handled. President Truman would waste little time to make sure that the war with Japan came to an end. As the battles in the Pacific raged on, President Truman ordered the Air Force to unleash the new A-bomb on the Japanese. While some politicians were against the use of this bomb, Truman knew that it was the only answer to stop the loss of American lives and end the war. On August 6, 1945 a squadron of B-29 Superfortress planes took off and dropped the first A-bomb on the city of Hiroshima. Three days later they dropped another A-bomb on Nagasaki literally wiping the two cities off the map. Six days later, on August 15, the Japanese would surrender. Victory was claimed by the U.S. and the war ended. VJ Day erupted all over the country in a very wild celebration everywhere coast to coast. The war was now completely over and people could really get back to normal again. As crazy as the celebrations were for VE Day, these topped it. All that was needed was the formal signing of surrender. That was accomplished less than a month later on September 2, 1945 aboard the *USS Missouri* as the Japanese, United States, led by General Douglas MacArthur and the allies: Great Britain, Canada, China, Australia, Soviet Union, New Zealand, and the Netherlands all signed the treaty. Families eagerly looked forward to the return home of fathers, husbands, brothers, sisters, friends and getting on with their lives. For those who lost family members during the war, and the sadness and loss it brought, they knew these men and women did not die in vain. It was a joyful time for every American knowing peace had come, families could be families again and enjoy a new and better life ahead. Returning veterans could take advantage of the new G.I. Bill that had been enacted in 1944 by FDR. After the formal surrender signing, in quick order President

Truman lifted the few remaining rationing and travel restrictions. This added another big plus to the lives of millions of people and the economy. Within weeks factories and plants were back to making cars, new products for the home and much more. Happy days were definitely here again.

When it came to the big bands they were still out playing at those venues still available, but the reception and crowds were a far cry from a few years earlier. No longer were places jam-packed, no longer were the band's few radio shows a "must listen", and record sales had taken a huge drop. More ballrooms had closed and one of the best known that had been *THE* place to go, shut its doors and became a furniture warehouse. The writing was on the wall, but still a few new bands popped up hoping to still capture some of that magic. Former Miller arranger **Jerry Gray** put a band together that was in the Miller style. Two trumpet players, **Billy Butterfield** and **Ralph Marterie** also put bands together and hit the road and would do okay for a short time. While it was tough going, the established names, **Goodman**, **Shaw**, **Dorsey**, **Herman**, and **Basie** were still holding on to their popularity and were still drawing on some success with their recordings. Still, even these mainstays saw and felt the change taking place musically. The vocalists continued to become more popular on radio, on personal appearances and their record sales were doing very well. One writer said at the time, *"Without the name Glenn Miller, the big band scene now just seemed empty."* But many reasoned even if Miller was still alive, he would have changed and gone into other areas of music he had planned on. The war was over, the country was moving

in a new direction looking toward an exciting and peaceful future, the past was just that, the past. Still there were a few more who felt they could buck the trend and make a difference. **Randy Brooks**, **Bob Chester**, and **Sam Donahue** were among them but whatever popularity they were able to muster was very short lived. The clubs, recording companies, theaters, and radio were fully aware of the change. No longer were there any big band radio shows, no remotes, no stage shows, recordings by big bands were few and not chart busters. Worst of all, places for bands to appear had dwindled down to a precious few.

After a happy and glorious holiday season with the war over, **1946** came with the country in a very good frame of mind. Family members home from the military resuming their regular lives, going to school, and getting jobs. Many were now moving out of the cities and to new places known as the suburbs. One of the largest developments of this new type living was Levittown, Long Island. Homes were being built everywhere there was land available, and sub divisions began to spring up all over. I remember when we moved from Jersey City out to the suburbs and a new development called Birchwood in the summer of 1945. All of the homes looked pretty much alike, 2-3 bedroom Cape Cod-styled homes with a basement and attic on a 75x100 plot with paved, tree-lined lighted streets, and it was like going to a new paradise. My folks paid the grand total of $4,800 for this "palace" that we would live in for the next 20 years. My years growing up in this new environment was something very special, as I am sure it was for others of my age and their families. So many new products, ideas, and looks to the future came on the American landscape in 1946. There was the introduction of the radial tire from Michelin. Electric blankets showed up in many homes for warm nights in bed. The Osterizer blender and Tupperware were new

items that became immediate hits with housewives, and Tide laundry detergent was something new that caught on with the homemaker. It was also the year the new entertainment medium called television would make its debut. When it was first introduced at the New York World's Fair in 1939-40, it was hailed by some as nothing more than a fad that wouldn't last. It was a product that would be too expensive for an average family to own. However, those with an eye and mind to the future saw it as both an entertainment and learning tool that would be an essential part of life. While television didn't have the big major impact in 1946, with about one million sets coast to coast, by the following year television would really begin to show how important it would become.

Radio was still king, even though it was going through some changes. People still tuned their radios into **Bob Hope**, **Jack Benny**, **Mel Blanc**, **The Fat Man**, **Gunsmoke**, **Twenty Questions**, **Groucho Marx**, and others. It was also the year that radio listeners were introduced to two young men who loved to make fun of current entertainment, something they would do for the next 50 years both on radio and TV, **Bob and Ray**. It was also at this time that the "disc jockey" was becoming more of a radio staple, and pioneers like **Martin Block**, **Al Jarvis**, **William B. Williams**, **Dick Whittinghill** and others would bring personality to radio while spinning records. This would open up a whole new chapter in radio in the coming decades. I became part of the disc jockey brigade in 1954. The movies in

1946 gave Hollywood one of its best years with great films like **The Yearling**, **Best Years of Our Lives**, **Razor's Edge**, **Duel in the Sun**, and **It's a Wonderful Life**. Summer became fun once again as families took family vacations, flocked to the beaches, the lakes, went on Sunday drives and had exciting times at amusement parks like **Coney Island**, **King's Park**, **Palisades Park**, **Kennywood**, **Knots Berry Farm**, **Cedar Point**, **Dorney Park**, **Rye Playland**, and many more all over the country. It was a time when kids were being kids again, families were families and with so many new products, inventions and promise coming in the post war years, it was a special time for young people growing up. It was truly amazing to see, in the space of one year, the changes that had taken place in the country. While several plants would become companies to work for our military by producing parts, new technology, etc., most were back in business doing what they had done prior to the war, only better and with more modern equipment. It would also soon open the door for some products coming from other countries to make their way into the American home and our way of life.

In spite of the big downfall the big band scene had taken, one more new band came on the scenes led by Ralph Flanagan. Hoping to cash in on the loss of Glenn Miller, the band was patterned almost exactly like his in every way. However, without permission from the Miller estate and threats of a lawsuit Flanagan was forced to change the style of his band. While Helen Miller and the Miller Estate wanted to see Glenn's music live on they wanted to make the choice of who would be the one to carry on the Miller tradition. They chose former Miller sax player and vocalist **Tex Beneke** to lead an authorized Miller band. As for the female singer in the band, Beneke auditioned and signed a young New York teenager by the name of **Eydie Gormé**. By now, it was the more well-known names of **Goodman**, **Dorsey**, etc., who were still doing okay. Now there were less than 100 ballrooms operating (down from a peak of over 650) coast to coast and even these big names were finding it difficult to keep audiences entertained. Two of the most popular in the New York-New Jersey area, **Frank Dailey's Meadowbrook** in Cedar Grove, N.J. and the **Glen Island Casino** in New Rochelle, N.Y., stopped bringing in big bands altogether. The Meadowbrook would totally change and become a dinner theater for a number of years before the

wrecking ball came along. The **Glen Island Casino** switched over to being just a restaurant and a catering hall.

By **1947**, there were some major changes with the band leaders. **Artie Shaw** had left the business to become a writer and get into book publishing, **Benny Goodman** went from a big band to a quartet and became much more involved with classical music, **Tommy Dorsey** semi-retired, but played various venues sparingly, using mostly pick-up musicians for band dates, **Harry James**, settled in Hollywood with his actress wife **Betty Grable**, radio and television would soon be the roost for **Ozzie Nelson**, while **Charlie Barnet** also semi-retired from the scene. **Larry Clinton** stepped away from the limelight for good in the late 40's never to return. **Woody Herman** dropped the big band and would front small jazz groups for a time before he retired. For most all of the others they

either just faded quietly out of sight, or found other areas of music or entertainment to get involved in.

Thanks to the ban back in 1942-43 that did not allow bands to record new songs and opened the door for singers and it paid off in their growing popularity. Most all of them, **Frank Sinatra**, **Jo Stafford**, Dinah Shore, **Dick Haymes**, **Peggy Lee**, **Doris Day**, **Vaughn Monroe** and others were doing well with hit records and some like Sinatra, Shore, Monroe also had very popular radio shows. A couple of other singers from the big bands, **Rosemary Clooney** and **Perry Como** would also soon begin to make their popularity known. There were other singers from the heyday of the big bands that would have very successful movie careers, like **Jane Russell**, **Betty Hutton**, **Janet Blair**, **Gloria De Haven** and let us not forget **Dale Evans**, who would become known as the "Queen of the West" with her marriage to cowboy star **Roy Rogers**. Nor can we ever forget vocalist **Harriet Hilliard**, who sang with the **Ozzie Nelson Orchestra** and was married to him. When the big band era fizzled they found a home on radio with their own show that would later become a staple of early television along with sons David and future rock star Ricky. Probably the most unlikely of all was a male singer with the **Horace Heidt Orchestra** who would become a household name on television and the movies, and best known for playing "Norton" on "The Honeymooners", **Art Carney**. There was also the **Charlie Spivak Orchestra** that began in 1939 and continued to do well. The drummer in Spivak's band would have a bigger career as a comedian in Las Vegas, clubs and later television. His name was **Charlie Callas**. In another twist of show business fate, a very talented sax player came out of the Navy in 1946 and joined the popular and long-running **Claude Thornhill Orchestra**. While he was a good musician, well liked and a fun guy, he would go on to become a household name in the early days of television for his all-out comedy style on his weekly Saturday night

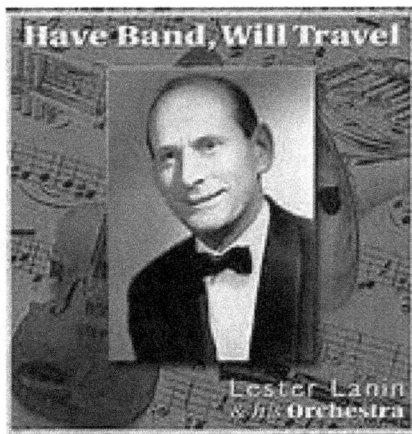

Have Band, Will Travel

Lester Lanin & his Orchestra

TV show. The former big band saxophonist's name was **Sid Caesar**.

However, as the big swing bands faded out of the scene by 1947, the

sweet bands of Guy Lombardo, **Freddy Martin** (his male singer was future TV star and entrepreneur **Merv Griffin**), **Sammy Kaye**, **Russ Morgan** and others of that style found audiences with a much older crowd eager to come and dance at the places these bands played. It was also a time when society music came back and orchestra leader **Lester Lanin** would lead that style for many years with his various mixes of instruments geared to a society beat. He would also have a series of very successful albums in the years ahead. When it came to the record charts in 1946 and 1947, except for a couple of the **Beneke/Miller** band records making the charts, it was dominated by the vocalists and vocal groups. There was no longer a need for the sound of the big bands in this new post-war world. Of course another wild hysterical time in music was less than 10 years away, when again music geared to the younger set would take over the air waves and record charts. The rock-and-roll era would be the next musical craze.

It was a valiant effort by everyone in the big band movement to try and keep it going, but with all the changes taking place as the country and the world moving ahead, there was no chance for this once great era to survive. Even the most respected music writers and critics knew the time had come after an extremely successful, profitable, life changing ten plus years. Though a few bands hung around for a short time before calling it quits, the bigger names were the only ones to still have some appeal and even they were not doing all that great. For the few who restarted a big band hoping to catch lightning in a bottle once more, it didn't work. Everything around us had changed and by the time 1947 arrived, the era of the big bands would become a very pleasant memory of the past to most.

Now it was television. In one year, the number had gone from one million to over ten million homes with black and white TV sets with 7", 10" and the "large" 12" screens. The networks had full programing on morning, noon and night with shows of every description. Some radio shows would make the move to television over the next few years and the ladies' favorites, the soap opera, also would move and become a staple of daytime television. That was just the beginning of this new medium. The entertainment, information and history it would bring into the American home would be unending. As television grew it became more than just entertainment and would forever change the way we lived and learned. Let it be noted the big band era came along at the perfect time in the country's growth and, thanks to the foresight of **Benny Goodman**, as well as the others, provided the people with one of the most exciting musical times during one of the toughest times in the country's history. For those who lived it, were part of it and remember it, the years between 1935 and 1947 will always remain very special in the history of this great country. It was a time *"When Swing Was King"*.

CHAPTER 5
1948 AND BEYOND
THE POST-WAR BIG BAND ERA

After the era of the big bands had come to a close it would be the late 1950's when another attempt of sorts would be made to recapture that sound. A new band headed up by former Charlie Spivak and Harry James musician *Les Elgart* had great success with a series of very danceable albums for Columbia Records. The albums were big sellers and the Elgart band was on the road playing mainly college campuses with excellent reaction by the young people. One interesting tidbit about the Elgart band. It was made up of the usual five saxes, four trumpets, three trombones, guitar, bass and drums, but NEVER used a piano! Thanks to great arrangements it was never missed. It is also interesting to note that one of the big Elgart hits, *"Bandstand Boogie"* would be used as the theme song for

"Dick Clark's American Bandstand" show right through its run into the 1980's. Also in the '50's, **Tex Beneke** had been replaced to lead the Miller band by former Miller drummer **Ray McKinley**. The Miller aggregation were kept very busy, doing as many as 250 dates a year with concerts and college campuses along with a series of bestselling albums for RCA Victor. Also in the '50's as rock-and-roll was taking over as **THE** music of the day, the **Dorsey Brothers** had patched up their differences to host a national weekly television show for the summer on CBS-TV called **"Stage Show"**. The show would only last one season because of illness. The show is noteworthy not only because of the two brothers returning, but also because a new young singer made his TV debut on that show by the name of **Elvis Presley**. Tommy Dorsey would pass away on November 26, 1956 at the age of 51. Jimmy, who was fighting cancer, still managed to have one more hit, the instrumental **"So Rare"** in 1957, before succumbing to the disease. Like Helen Miller, Jane Dorsey owned the rights to Tommy's band and name and had trombonist **Warren Covington** take over the Dorsey band after his death. After Covington, **Sam Donahue** took over until 1961 when the band was under the leadership of trombonist **Buddy Morrow** until his death in 2010. After Morrow's death a series of former sidemen would lead the Dorsey orchestra and still do to this day playing various venues around the country.

In the 1960's, two bands from across the pond, **Ted Heath** coming from the UK and band leader **Bert Kaempfert** coming from Germany, tried to do their part, with a lot of success, to

revive the sound of the big bands. Ted Heath's band was a more traditional big swing band and had a series of top-selling albums for London Records. Heath recreated dozens of the hit songs from the big band era, partly using the original arrangements with some twists of his own that made them not only listenable, but very danceable. He also did several tours of the States to good receptions, with many college-age young people hearing the big band sound for the first time. Kaempfert, on the other hand, used a big band sound but also with a chorus of singers who also acted as instruments. He would also have a series of successful album for Decca Records, but appealed to an older age group. While it was some 20 years later there were still those who loved the music and wanted to hear it again. There was also a new generation getting their first taste of what their moms and dads used to listen and dance to. It didn't end with those revivals from the '50's and the '60's with **Elgart**, **Heath**, **Kaempfert** and a couple of others who

made similar attempts. It would continue on into the next decade as well with a major record label coming up with a great idea.

In the 1970's, **Capitol Records** coaxed band leader **Glen Gray** out of retirement to create and lead a series of albums recreating the big band sound of all the various bands playing their hits and theme songs. Gray personally handpicked the very best musicians in Hollywood and New York, many of whom had played with the big bands back in the day. Gray and Capitol would wind up releasing a series of very successful albums of the big band sound. So successful was the series, that Gray and Capitol decided to take it one step further by releasing several albums of the current songs of the day and how they would sound if they had

been done in the *Miller, Goodman, Shaw, James, Herman, Dorsey*, etc. style. These were also best sellers and brought back that sound for a time and again to a new generation. Capitalizing on this success, Gray also would do an album for Capitol recreating the great hits of his own big band from the '30's and '40's. It was very obvious from one decade to the next that while this music from this very special era may have left, there would always be someone to bring back the sound and the

memories of that music. It is a music style that will never die and always be a part of the fabric that makes up the American music blanket, simply because it IS America's music.

At the present time, only the *Duke Ellington* and *Tommy Dorsey* bands, under the direction of former big band players are out working the tour schedule to some degree. However, the busiest of them all, and not surprisingly, is the *Glenn Miller Orchestra* who have continually played nonstop since Miller's death in 1944. After those holiday broadcasts from Paris in 1944 the band was formed as a co-op unit and continued to play until they were discharged from the service. Then as we mentioned above, under the Miller estate run by Miller's widow Helen, *Tex Beneke* would lead the first post war incarnation of the band. After a falling out with the estate he was replaced by *Ray McKinley* who took over the band in the late '50's through the '70's before ill health caused McKinley to retire. All through that time and bestselling albums the Miller band was doing 200- 250 dates a year, coast to coast. After McKinley retired the Miller band was led by *Buddy De Franco, Peanuts Hucko, Buddy Morrow*, and in 1981 *Larry O'Brien*, with his extensive big band background took over the leadership role which he would do for the next 30 years. O'Brien retired in 2011 and turned over the Miller baton to *Nick Hilscher*, who had been part of the current Miller group. Today in 2015, the *Glenn Miller Orchestra*, some

71 years after Miller's passing, is still the most popular band in the world. They average close to 300 concert dates a year throughout the U.S. and Canada from their home base located in Lake Mary, Florida, which is just outside Orlando. Check their website www.glennmillerorchestra.com for their tour schedule and a lot more.

There is more that even longtime fans of Glenn Miller may not be aware of.

Ray McVay   Wil Salden

The **Glenn Miller Orchestra** is the only band from the big band/swing era licensed to operate elsewhere in the world. The previous photos are of **Wil Salden**, who leads the authorized Miller band out of the Netherlands and plays up to 300 dates a year all throughout Europe, plus having their own recordings. The other photo is **Ray McVay**, who leads the Miller band in Great Britain and the British Isles, doing over 200 dates a year and also recordings. Both bands play the exact charts, emulate the same style of Miller showmanship, wear the same style band uniforms, carry the same male, female vocalists, and a vocal group fashioned after the **Modernaires**, called the **Moonlight Serenaders**. Both groups have great websites also. I was totally amazed when I first listened and watched videos of both of these authorized bands. I have listened to and heard a number of Miller imitators over the years, but the three Miller authorized units by the Miller estate in the U.S., Europe and the British Isles have it nailed perfectly in every way.

I have no doubt in my mind that Mr. Miller is smiling down, giving a big thumbs up to **Nick Hilscher**, **Wil Salden**, and **Ray McVay**. They are doing a fantastic job carrying on his name, his memory, his legacy, and with the greatest of respect, his music to millions worldwide each and every year.

CHAPTER 6
YOU'RE ON THE AIR!

Throughout this book, I have referred to the importance of radio to the big band/swing era, and it was a big factor in its popularity. However, the use of the bands were not only relegated to the late-night "dance party" type band shows the networks presented during the big band era. There is much more to it and a lot of it had begun before the big band scene would even get underway.

Back in the early '30's, circa 1932-33 the **Gus Arnheim Orchestra** presented a weekly coast to coast radio show **"This is the Coconut Grove"** from the famed Hollywood venue. It was also Arnheim who would introduce singer **Bing Crosby** to nationwide audiences through his band and show. Another orchestra leader who made it big in radio prior to the band shows was **Horace Heidt**. He was on a different level, while not totally a dance band, it

was more of a show band with 16 musicians and a glee club, plus solo singers and musicians. He came into prominence with two radio shows, the first in 1935, the *"Horace Heidt for Alemite Show"*. His second radio show which began in 1938 was *"Pot Of Gold"*, the first radio giveaway show, where unsuspecting callers would have a chance to win $1,000 (a huge sum back then). The show was so successful it spun off into a movie with Heidt and the entire musical aggregation appearing in it.

There were several other bands that had their own shows long before radio would play a very significant role in the rise and growth of the big band/swing era. Among them was the **Freddy Martin Orchestra** (the male vocalist in the band was **Merv Griffin**) who did several different sponsored radio shows from Los Angeles. In 1936 the **Jimmy Dorsey Orchestra** band was on the **Bing Crosby** radio show. From 1933 through 1937, the **Glen Gray Orchestra** was one of the mainstays of a variety show called the *"Camel Caravan"*. There was the sweet sound of the **Art Kassel Orchestra** that was based out of Chicago and his weekly *"Elgin Watch Show"* in the early 30's that was a radio mainstay. (Before going on his own Benny Goodman put in time with this band). **Jan Savitt** was another band leader who did very well with his orchestra that

featured a "shuffle rhythm". He had a very successful radio show on CBS called *"Rhapsody in Rhythm"* that came out of Philadelphia and helped his band secure a lot of big ballroom and club dates during the era. Another sweet band who did well on radio with a unique approach was the **Sammy Kaye Orchestra**. As radio shows back then were played in front of a live studio audience, Kaye came up with an audience participation idea where people would be selected to lead the Kaye band in a song, the winner determined by audience applause. This created the very popular radio show *"So You Want to Lead a Band"*. The radio version got redone and moved to television years later but without the same success. Another innovative leader, who we mentioned earlier in the book was **Kay Kyser**, whose band played some solid dance music, but his gimmick, **"Kyser's Kollege of Musical Knowledge"** was a huge hit both on his radio show of the same name and in person. Kyser would dress up in cap and gown and give out musical questions to audience members and the right answers got small prizes, if they missed they got a "razzberry" from the band. There were many other bands that had local weekly radio shows that emanated out of New York, Boston, Chicago, Detroit, Los Angeles, and other cities where the bands were based.

There was one other area where the big bands and radio variety shows came together and gave the bands an even further push. That was when some radio stars signed these bands to be their shows musical backdrop. For example, the **Skinnay Ennis Orchestra** was featured on the **"Abbott and Costello"** show, **Harry James** on the **"Danny Kaye Show"**, **Ray Noble** was on the **"Edgar Bergen & Charlie McCarthy Show"**, **Charlie Spivak's Orchestra** was, for several years, part of the **"Kate Smith Show"**, the **Anson Weeks Orchestra** in the 1930's (their popularity was helped by being part of the **"Eddie Cantor Camel Show"**), and also the **Ted Weems Orchestra**, who was the musical addition to the popular **"Fibber McGee and Molly Show"** among others. There were many more who were all part of radio's connection to the big bands. Then there was also **Ozzie Nelson** whose band was on the **"Bob Ripley Show"** and of course later they would have their own radio show, **"The Adventures of Ozzie and Harriet"** that later, as sons David and Ricky grew up, would become a TV hit. The radio connection would not be complete without adding the very successful marriage of the **"Bob Hope Show"** and the very popular **Les Brown Orchestra**. This would be a union lasting into the 1980's through radio, USO tours and television. Just about every hit radio show that was hosted by stars like **Jack Benny**, **Fred Allen**, **Red Skelton**, and

others used one of the big bands as their featured musical part of the show. In some cases, besides playing music, the leaders actually would take part in some of the skits on the shows. One more show we should mention began back in the 1930's and transcended four decades from radio to television was *"Your Hit Parade"* where the Top 10 songs of each week were performed by a variety of artists.

So while many of these bands had been on radio before the big band/swing era began, there is no question how big a part radio played. When the networks finally decided to go one step further with the big band only shows like *"Saturday Swing Session"*, *"Camel Caravan"*, *"Coca Cola Swing Club"*, *"Chesterfield Supper Club"*, *"Old Gold Dance Party"* and others that were presented, it was more than enough for lovers of the music to listen to on the radio. It was also during this period that some of the stations in the bigger cities would have announcers playing records on the air a couple of hours during the daytime hours, sometimes in between the airing of the "soap operas". It was not unusual for the women to be tuned into *"The Romance of Helen Trent"* and when the show ended some very proper talking announcer would spin some records of the various bands. The announcers had perfect diction, were very staid and void of personality but they would become the earliest version of the radio disc jockey that would really come into vogue in the late 1940's and into the 1950's and beyond.

CHAPTER 7

THE BIG BANDS & ROCK-AND-ROLL

Some 8 or 10 years after the death of the big band era, the newest craze, rock-and-roll, came in and took over as the music of the youth of the '50's. While there was a lot of "shake, rattle and roll" going on and the discovery of **Elvis Presley** and new songwriters putting out all kinds of rock-and-roll ditties, there was also something else. A lot of these groups and the record labels didn't forget about some of the great songs from the big band era and had them redone as rock-and-roll hits. While many who listened to rock-and-roll may have thought these were new songs, those big band hits now being performed rock-and-roll style were first recorded and popular before most of those teens were born!

Here are just a few examples: **Fats Domino** had a Top 5 hit in 1956

with a song titled *"Blueberry Hill"*. The fact? It was a #1 hit for the *Glenn Miller Orchestra* in 1939 with the vocal done by *Ray Eberle*. In 1958, *Billy Ward & the Dominos* had a big Top 10 hit with *"Stardust"* that was originally a top hit in 1938 by the *Artie Shaw Orchestra*. In 1944, the *Claude Thornhill Orchestra* (Fran Warren doing the vocal) had a big Top 10 hit with *"Sunday Kind of Love"*. In 1954, it hit the rock-and-roll charts by *The Harptones*. In 1959, Ernie Fields went to #1 on the charts with *"In the Mood"* which was a #1 hit for *Glenn Miller* in 1939. In 1956, *The Platters* had a Top 5 hit with the song *"Twilight Time"*, that originally was a hit in 1945 for the *Les Brown Orchestra* and the vocal by *Doris Day*. There were many more that went from big band chart hits to rock-and-roll hits. Probably the oldest of all was a big hit song from 1935, recorded by the *Guy Lombardo Orchestra*, and 21 years later was a major hit once again in 1956. The song we refer to was *"Goody, Goody"*, recorded by *Frankie Lyman and the Teenagers*. So even at the height of the rock-and-roll craze, songs from the big bands were not forgotten but recreated with respect, a new beat, a new style and a new audience. As we mentioned, there were a vast number of songs from the big band era that were redone during the height of rock-and-roll in the '50's and '60's bringing the songs to a whole new audience. This even carried through into the 1970's and '80's when there were remakes of big hits from the big band era.

It was just further proof, and continues to this day, that the music from the big band/swing era has stood the test of time over and over again. It may be a different time on the calendar, but in some fashion, and in some musical way, many of the songs from that historical and special era will always be with us.

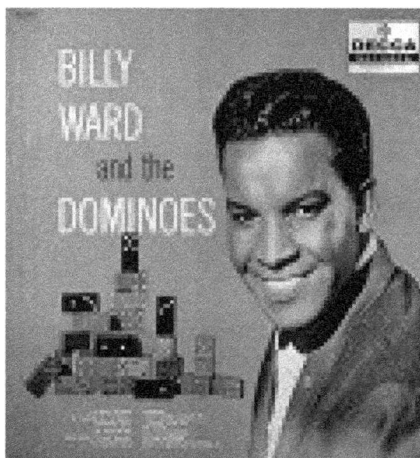

CHAPTER 8
ONE FINAL NOTE

While I centered on many of the bigger names: **Miller**, **Goodman**, **Shaw**, **James**, **Clinton**, **Dorsey**, **Herman**, etc. as the driving force and among the most prolific during the era, there were many others. So many bands made contributions to the era, both big and small, helping to make this period so special. Those contributions came by way of not-so-well-known leaders, sidemen, arrangers, songwriters, regional names, but all were part of this historic time in American music. It will never be recaptured like it was, but will also never be forgotten. Listed here are some other bands who were part of this incredible era: **Bix Beiderbecke, Art Kassel, Benny Carter, Will Bradley, Ray Anthony, Erskine Hawkins, Art Cook, Dean Hudson, Bobby Byrne, Clyde McCoy, Isham Jones, Dolly Dawn, Elliot Lawrence, Shep Fields, Frankie Carle, Billy May, Red Nichols, Russ Carlyle, Boyd Raeburn, Horace Heidt, Teddy Powell, Stan Kenton, Red Norvo, Sam Donahue, Wayne King, Tommy Tucker, Ina Ray Hutton, Buddy Morrow, Lucky Millender, Tony Pastor, Sauter-Finnegan, Johnny Long, Andy Kirk, Bob Chester, Sonny Dunham, Lee Castle, Tony Pastor, Eddy Duchin, Si Zentner, Bobby Sherwood, Blue Barron, Russ Morgan, Frank Dailey, Henry Busse,**

Xavier Cugat, Lou Breese, Raymond Scott, Mal Hallett, Orin Tucker, Jan Garber, Bob Zurke, Don Glasser, Freddie Slack, Happy Felton, Billy May, Art Mooney, Tiny Hill, Henry Jerome, Ted Mack, Buddy Clarke, Jack Teagarden, Billy Butterfield, Richard Maltby, Ziggy Elman, Skinnay Ennis, Randy Brooks, and many more who all made contributions to the big band/swing era in some way.

CHAPTER 9

IN CLOSING

In closing, being raised in this era and having a father who was part of it as a musician and band leader, I was fortunate to get to listen and enjoy that music as a youngster. I got a very early education on the music, what went into it, how it was done, how it was received, and what it meant to people. While I never learned to play a musical instrument, it was this love of music that helped me in my career in radio for more than 20 years. Now, close to 70 years after the era had passed, this great music can still be heard electronically, on CDs, live performances, and through nostalgic TV specials. While so much of today's music will be forgotten in a few years, the music of the big bands will still be remembered and heard, and will always remain the greatest musical era in the history of American music.

I have tried, through this book, to not only give you a peek into the world of the big band/swing era, but also how life was in the U.S. back then. I tried to capture the feel and essence of what it was like to go through the post-Depression years in the country and then the time of WW II and after, and hope that I succeeded. This book was a true labor of love for me and I hope you enjoy taking this trip back in time as much as I did researching it and putting it all together. May music always fill your heart and soul. My sincere thanks to you for getting this book.

Art Koch

PHOTO GALLERY

Photos

Pg. 1 — Benny Goodman **Pg.** 2 — Benny Goodman Palomar **Pg.** 3 — Glen Gray Orchestra **Pg.** 4 — Dorsey Brothers **Pg.** 5 — Tommy Dorsey Orchestra, Kay Kyser Orchestra **Pg.** 6 — Fibber McGee & Molly, Roseland **Pg.** 7 — Meadowbrook **Pg.** 8 — Duke Ellington Orchestra, Adolf Hitler **Pg.** 9 — FDR **Pg.** 10 — Ozzie Nelson, Charlie Barnet, Artie Shaw **Pg.** 11 — Ray Noble Orchestra, Glenn Miller Orchestra **Pg.** 12 — Look Magazine, Lincoln Tunnel **Pg.** 13 —Edgar Bergen & Charlie McCarthy **Pg.** 15 — Aragon Ballroom **Pg.** 16 — Orson Welles, War of the Worlds **Pg.**17 — Superman **Pg.** 18 — Les Brown Orchestra **Pg.** 19 — Lena Horne, Glenn Miller Orchestra **Pg.** 20 — Glenn Miller Glen Island Casino **Pg.** 21 — Glenn Miller Story Movie **Pg.** 22 — Band Bus **Pg.** 23 — — Carnegie Hall Ticket, Benny Goodman **Pg.** 24 — Goodman Concert LP **Pg.** 25 — Larry Clinton **Pg.** 26 — Glenn Miller Orchestra, *Swing Magazine* **Pg.** 27 — Paul Whiteman **Pg.** 28 — Harry James Orchestra **Pg.** 29 — New York World's Fair **Pg.** 30 — Uncle Sam Poster **Pg.** 31 — Dairy Queen **Pg.** 32 — Helen O'Connell & Bob Eberly **Pg.** 33 — Ozzie Nelson Orchestra, Les Brown & Doris Day **Pg.** 34 — Elitch Gardens Ballroom **Pg.** 37 — Edward R. Murrow, USO **Pg.** 38 — ASCAP **Pg.** 39 — Sun Valley

Serenade Movie Poster **Pg.** 40 — 1941 Pontiac **Pg.** 41 — Newspaper Headline **Pg.** 42 — Kearney, N.J. Shipyards **Pg.** 43 — Actor Clark Gable **Pg.** 44 — B-24 Aircraft Factory **Pg.** 45 — Orchestra Wives Movie Poster **Pg.** 46 — James C. Petrillo, Frank Sinatra **Pg.** 47 — Glenn Miller AAF Band **Pg.** 48 — Women in the Factory **Pg.** 49 — Women's Professional Baseball **Pg.** 50 — Detroit Riots **Pg.** 51 — Detroit Riots **Pg.** 52 — Army Nurses, Women AAF Pilots **Pg.** 53 — B-25 Bombing Tokyo, Normandy Landing **Pg.** 54 — Ration Books, Roller Derby **Pg.** 55 — Ballrooms before and after **Pg.** 56 — Glenn Miller AAF Band **Pg.** 57 — Obituary for Glenn Miller **Pg.** 60 — FDR Funeral Procession, President Harry S. Truman **Pg.** 61 — Martin Block **Pg.** 62 — Japan signing surrender **Pg.** 63 — Randy Brooks Orchestra, Ralph Marterie Band **Pg.** 64 — Moving into the suburbs **Pg.** 65 — TV set, Coney Island **Pg.** 66 — Tex Beneke **Pg.** 67 — Art Carney, Claude Thornhill Orchestra **Pg.** 68 — Lester Lanin **Pg.** 69 — TV set **Pg.** 71 — Les Elgart Orchestra **Pg.** 72 — Dorsey Brothers & Elvis Presley **Pg.** 73 — Bert Kaempfert, Ted Heath, Glen Gray Album **Pg.** 74 — World Famous Glenn Miller Orchestra **Pg.** 75 — Wil Salden, Ray McVay **Pg.** 77 — Horace Heidt **Pg.** 78 — Sammy Kaye Orchestra **Pg.** 79 — Les Brown, Doris Day, Bob Hope **Pg.** 81 — Artie Shaw **Pg.** 82 — Billy Ward and the Dominos

ABOUT THE AUTHOR

Art Koch was born in 1935 in Brooklyn, New York and raised in Jersey City and East Paterson, New Jersey His father was a professional musician who played saxophone and clarinet with several bands and had his own band during the big band/swing era. Art attended Lodi High School in N.J., graduating in 1953, and spent 4 years in the Air Force in Special Services. After the Air Force, he entered radio as a disc jockey, a position he would hold on and off at various stations over the next 24 years. He has also worked in promotion for Decca Records, in management for the Sam Goody retail record store chain, co-produced country music concerts and shows in the New York-New Jersey area, and Florida and had his own talent management firm, Warrick Productions, for several years.

He married in 1958, divorced in 1965, and from that marriage had two sons, Warren and Eric. From 1969 to 2002, he was married to Florence "Flo" Auer until she passed away from complications due to a massive stroke and Alzheimer's. In 2009, he met Carole Tutko, who is now his partner in life. Since 1989, Mr. Koch has been a writer, editor, and film critic for P.A.C. Magazine Publishing Company in Palm Harbor, Florida, writing on a variety of subjects, sports, entertainment, movies, music, food and other subjects. In October 2014, Mr. Koch was presented with a Lifetime Achievement Award by *NightMoves Magazine*.

With an extensive big band record and CD collection, plus his years in radio, his music tastes are extremely varied. However, being raised in the era, the big band and swing sound of the 1930's and 1940's hold a very special place in the author's heart. This book is something he has wanted to do for a number of years and finally brought it to fruition as a true labor of love.

The Entrepreneur's Publisher

RICHTER
PUBLISHING